VISION
A NEW
OF BOARD LEADERSHIP

John Carver and Miriam Mayhew
Introduction by George E. Potter

A New Vision of Board Leadership: Governing the Community College
by John Carver and Miriam Mayhew

Published by:
Association of Community College Trustees
1740 "N" Street, NW
Washington, DC 20036

A Special Project of the ACCT Trust Fund

Library of Congress Catalog Card Number: 94-79288

ISBN 1-886237-01-8

Printed in the United States of America

I t would be rare indeed to find a more important or more difficult role, carried out by more dedicated, selfless public servants, than that of a governing board member of a community college. With all of the passion and ability we possess, each of us undertakes the responsibility to represent our fellow citizens, and in full view of the often critical, self-interested public, exercise control over a highly complex organization in an uncertain economic and social environment, fulfill a mission that speaks to improving the quality of life, and lest we forget, demonstrate that we have been successful!

Yet with all its importance and complexity, it would be difficult to find a role that is less clearly defined or that has less information and guidance to describe how it can best be performed.

The principles of good governance have been known for decades. Studies of college and university governing boards, including that of Clarke Kerr and Marian Gade (Association of Governing Boards of Universities and Colleges, 1989), have consistently shown that effective boards focus on overall policy and performance of the organization — strategic leadership — and delegate to the president the responsibility for management.

Unfortunately, most of those who have worked with and on governing boards have discovered that they spend little time fulfilling this leadership role and instead spend more of their time dealing with management issues and minutiae. As John Carver would state it, "By participating directly in the work of the organization, the board tends to become lost in the trees and to lose sight of the forest." This occurs, he believes, because "moving mountains an inch often appears less active than moving molehills a mile. Boards who would be strategic leaders must move at a more deliberate pace than their staffs, but with issues far more momentous."

The problem lies in the fact that while the principles of effective governance seem clear, we have lacked a good model with which to frame them and thus carry out our responsibilities.

In creating the "Policy Governance" model, Dr. Carver has made a significant contribution toward the improvement of governance of public and private nonprofit organizations. Through his writing, speaking, and workshops he has introduced his model to thousands of governing board members. He has challenged us to substantially reduce our involvement in "staff work" and concentrate our efforts on leadership, the result being not only a greater impact on the college itself, but most importantly, on the people the college serves.

There are several significant differences between traditional practice and "Policy Governance." Under the model, the board rather than looking inward, focusing on the institution for the issues with which it deals, shifts to an outward focus, looking at the community. With this outward focus, the board spends most of its time determining what benefit the community, which includes students, is to receive from the college.

Traditionally, the board spends most of its time dealing with the past or the present. Boards hear reports on past events, deciding to approve what has been or soon will be done. "Policy Governance" looks to the future. Boards create the vision, set goals, and establish desired outcomes. The model rejects the practice of the president setting the board's agenda, including meeting agendas. The board becomes proactive, rather than reactive, creating its own agenda, deciding the issues it will address, becoming obsessed with outcomes, rather than operations. In traditional practice, board decisions relate to staff "means," rather than "ends" policy. The clearest example of ends policy is the college mission itself, one of many outcome-oriented policies that express the values and vision of the board.

Beyond these, the model calls for board policy that addresses the board's responsibility and criteria for measurement of institutional performance.

Adopting the "Policy Governance" model takes a major commitment to relearn how we govern. In this book, John Carver and Miriam Mayhew have taken the model and related it specifically to community college governance. They explain clearly and concisely how the model can work for us. This book is *must* reading for all community college trustees and presidents. As trustees, we should be pleased that the

Association of Community College Trustees, our organization, can provide this excellent resource with the support of the ACCT Trust Fund.

For those boards wishing to implement the model, other available resources include: John Carver's *Boards That Make a Difference* and other publications (see Resources at the end of the book), ACCT's videotape of his presentation at the 1993 Annual Convention, ACCT's Board Retreat Service, sessions at ACCT conventions and seminars, and information from community college colleagues who are already using the model.

There is great opportunity here—opportunity to provide true leadership and to facilitate excellence in operation. I encourage you to take the challenge, to take the next step in leading our Community College Movement by improving the quality of governance at your college.

George E. Potter
Trustee
Jackson Community College
Jackson, Michigan

The subject of effective community college governance has become increasingly important. Community colleges, like most other organizations, have concentrated on improved management, improved teaching, even improved building maintenance and computerization of records. A few stalwart voices have been heard proclaiming that the board function itself is just as critical and just as in need of close scrutiny and improvement. George Potter, who introduces this book, certainly comes to mind in that regard, for he has been a voice for effective trusteeship since before it was popular.

Although not always as flexible and forward thinking as community colleges, many other institutions and organizations have been undergoing a similar shift from governance-as-usual to governance as a search for strategic leadership. We are in the business of bringing a transformation to boards of all types, from trade associations, to hospitals, to public education, to business corporations, and everything in between. We can do that because we have found that at its base, governance is possessed of some powerful and relatively simple principles. Simple though they might be, these principles have the rigor to literally transform our tired, though tradition-blessed, ideas of what boards are and how they function.

The senior author created in the mid-1970s a conceptual basis for a re-invented governance, one he called Policy Governance[SM]. He chose the name because the new technology enables a board to control, direct, inspire, and lead an organization solely through the explication of certain types of policies. This differs from "leading" by scrutinizing staff documents and plans, combing through budget details, being "involved" with staff, hearing reports on operational activities and all the other, traditionally pursued ways of governing. Beginning as a radical concept, the idea slowly gained a following until in the mid-1990s the Policy Governance model, now said to be sweeping North America, is being introduced in Europe. Both authors consult regularly with boards trying to convert governance-past into governance-future. We have seen first hand how easy and how difficult, how frustrating, and how rewarding the governance development task can be.

The Policy Governance model capitalizes on the generic similarity in governing board responsibilities across a vast and dissimilar array of types of organizations. But we recognize it to be equally true that hospital boards, social service boards, regulatory boards, trade association boards, and community college boards each face a different set of challenges. Indeed, one need not leave the community college family to find striking contrasts. Community colleges are by no means alike. Colleges differ in how board members are chosen, whether elected or appointed, and from what walks of life. They differ in the statutory framework their respective legislatures have laid down for them. Surrounding systems and pressures, that is, the organizational environments, present different interactions and relationships. Great differences exist in the generosity of government funding from one jurisdiction to another.

In describing a model of governance, then, we are forced to explain the abstractions and concepts, leaving to each board the task of applying principles to its own circumstances. We ask the reader's indulgence as we use "staff" to refer to staff and faculty, just as we repeatedly refer to "community" college rather than "technical" or "technical and community" college. We use the title "president" to refer to the chief executive officer, though perhaps we are on firmer ground with the majority of institutions with that choice. As is usually the case, the reader must work as hard as the writers and we heartily invite you to the task.

This work is divided into three sections. The first conveys in brief form the Policy Governance™ conceptual model for community college trustees. The second illustrates a number of factors in implementing the model in a community college. The third consists of interviews with community college trustees about their questions and concerns regarding the new approach.

We hope this book, encouraged and published by the Association of Community College Trustees, becomes a helpful tool for all community college trustees. We enjoy our ongoing relationship with the community college movement and with the trustees and administrative leaders who infuse the movement with such vigor and hope. We are particularly thankful to Ray Taylor, Sally Hutchins, and the ACCT staff for their support and guidance during this undertaking.

John Carver
Miriam Mayhew
Toronto, Ontario
August 1994

JOHN CARVER, said to be "the most provocative authority on governing boards," has become arguably the world's most published author on the topic. His book, *Boards That Make a Difference*, has outsold all other nonprofit and public administration texts among Jossey-Bass titles. His governance paradigm has spread across North America and is becoming recognized in Europe and Australia. John Carver earned bachelors and masters degrees at the University of Tennessee and a Ph.D. at Emory University, Atlanta. As an independent consultant, he operates as Carver Governance Design, Inc., in Carmel, Indiana, and as Carver Governance Canada, Ltd., in Toronto, Ontario. John, an American citizen, is a resident of Toronto.

MIRIAM MAYHEW learned the hard way that governance and governing boards require improvement. As the CEO of organizations in the public sector, and as a board member of voluntary organizations in Canada, she experienced the waste and damage which result from boards that fail to govern in a conceptually coherent manner. A governance consultant working with boards wishing to learn and use the Policy Governance model, she has been involved in the development of the governance capacity of boards in education, health, social service, associations, and charitable organizations. Miriam Mayhew grew up in England and received her bachelors degree from the University of East Anglia. After moving to Canada, she received her masters degree from Wilfrid Laurier University in Ontario. As an independent consultant, Ms. Mayhew operates as Miriam Mayhew Consulting, Toronto. Miriam is a resident of Toronto.

Dr. Carver and Ms. Mayhew are also co-authors of a forthcoming book from Jossey-Bass on the redesign of corporate governance.

A New Vision of Trustee Leadership

You are a community college trustee. You may have been one for a long time or you may have just joined the board. In either event, you are probably aware that an important trust has been placed in you. You are a member of a group of individuals authorized to govern a large, costly, complex organization for which a heterogeneous community and several levels of government have conflicting expectations. Whether a veteran or a new member of the board, you are acutely aware of your responsibilities and liabilities.

You may wonder how you can be all that you should be as a trustee and still have time for the rest of your life. Board members have a lot to be concerned about; each has his or her own list of worries. If you are a new trustee, your list of concerns may look different from the list of a veteran, but everyone has a worry list. Seasoned trustees may have developed ways of dealing with some of the worries, while the new trustee still has to establish those techniques.

This book is for you as a community college trustee. It has several aims. It will discuss the enormity and importance of the trustee's job. It will confirm something that trustees, and indeed most members of most governing boards have long suspected: that the job of the board is poorly defined and as presently practiced, largely incomprehensible. It will propose a new, different, coherent theory of board leadership called Policy Governance that improves the functioning and output of the board of trustees. Unlike much of the material available to boards, Policy Governance is not a series of tips. Rather, the model redesigns the job of the board of trustees in such a way as to ensure that the board leads powerfully on behalf of the public, and that the staff is enabled to act with as much authority as possible, though within limits set by the board.

You are likely to have joined the board of trustees of your community college because of some dearly held beliefs about community colleges, as well as about education in general. You probably have a vision about how you would like your community to be and how you would like the college to be a part of that vision. People usually join boards for these sorts of reasons. Inevitably, however, when they become board members, they discover that community, vision, and big picture issues are seldom discussed. Trustees find that far from designing the future, they have inherited a morass of micromanagement.

It is generally not trustees who cause traditional board process to be ineffective. Trustees invariably want to make a meaningful and substantial contribution to the governance of the college. *It is the traditional board process itself that is the culprit here.* Governance as we have known it was not consciously planned, but has been handed down over the decades. (It can be argued that no one would ever plan board process to resemble the way it has evolved.) Trustees find that they are compelled to burrow into the minutiae of staff plans, oversee purchases which adults routinely make in their personal lives quite without assistance, and make judgements of performance with no prior criteria having been established. Trustees find that while they don't want to meddle, there appears to be no way to act responsibly without seeming to meddle. The alternative, rubber stamping, is a frequent practice, but board members never feel completely comfortable with it, as well they should not.

Many trustees are perplexed about their role, and are hard pushed to define how the role of the board differs from the role of the management. They receive only spotty assistance from reference material in determining what their job is. In few other jobs do we define the contribution of the supervisor as identical to that of the supervisee, yet the tasks traditionally assigned to boards have led them to act largely as if they are staff "one step removed" or "superstaff". Board agendas commonly display this belief. For example, it is usual for the agenda (which has been put together by the staff) to be full of items of staff responsibility, such as the purchase of a vehicle or computer system, determination of a personnel issue, or details of a budget. Governance often appears to be little more than peering over staff shoulders.

It does not take long for new trustees to realize that their board does little that looks like leading, but does a great deal that looks like trying to keep up. This book will suggest to you that *leadership is not expressed by keeping up*. Indeed, "keeping up" is an insufficient goal for boards to pursue. Boards must be informed about a variety of issues in the organization in order to lead knowledgeably, it is true, so keeping up with some issues is important. But it is clear that there is some confusion on even the best boards about *what is to be kept up with*.

Many conscientious board members feel that in order to be responsible they must keep up with everything. Policy Governance proposes that while doubtless all of the activities, details, issues, and questions in a community college are important to someone, what is important to the board is different from what is important at levels below the board. The model will help you to distinguish the matters about which trustees must be leaders from those which don't matter at a governance level.

The Policy Governance model will suggest ways of clearly delegating to your president and how to treat her or him as a chief executive officer (CEO), the single link through which authority is delegated from the governing board to management. It will also propose an efficient way to set expectations and monitor them. But most of all, this model will exhort you to move on with the real business of the board of trustees: *leading* the community college on behalf of your community.

CHAPTER ONE

The Principles of Policy Governance

Policy Governance is a complete model for governance. That is, it is a coherent framework of concepts and principles that is internally consistent as well as powerful in dealing with whatever practical situations arise. Because it is a new approach to conceiving of the board's important job, its principles and concepts are unfamiliar to many trustees, including experienced ones. To make the most of this powerful model, it is best to fully understand its internal wholeness first, and only then attempt to apply it to the "real world" problems and challenges in your own college. The story of Policy Governance will be told by recounting the basic principles upon which it is built.

PRINCIPLE 1 The Trust in Trusteeship

The board of a nonprofit or public organization exists to represent the ownership of the organization in the same way as the board of a business corporation. In the case of a community college, ownership is a moral and often a legal concept. The ownership group is in many cases a local community, region, or state. (In associations, such as the Association of Community College Trustees, *members* are the owners.) Policy Governance recognizes foremost, then, that boards exist to *own the organization* on behalf of some identifiable public to which they are answerable, regardless of how rarely in practice boards hear from that public.

We can weaken this leadership obligation by referring to trustees as "volunteers". True, volunteers are people who are not paid for their services. To that extent, trustees are volunteers, but their unpaid status tells us nothing about the uniqueness of the role of trustees—and may even confuse it. For instance, we conventionally view volunteers as people who are there to help. This is not true of trustees. They are not there to help so much as to fulfill a more powerful role as voice of the ownership. This form of ownership could be referred to as a kind of "civic trusteeship."

Because this trusteeship forms the very foundation of governance, the *primary* relationship the community college board of trustees must establish, maintain, clarify, and protect is its relationship with its "owners", the community, and not, as so often is assumed, with staff, students, or faculty. These groups are extremely important, to be sure, and are usually part of the ownership themselves. But they are not the ownership *per se*, at most comprising only very visible subsets of it.

PRINCIPLE 2 The Board Speaks With One Voice or None At All

Despite the board's authoritative trusteeship, individual trustees have no authority over the college in their own right. The expression of trustee authority can only be in the context of the board as a whole.

Although this book is addressed to trustees, you will notice as you read on that it rarely refers to the individual trustee, though regularly to the board itself. The reason is simple: the board is the repository of an obligation of moral trusteeship, one which can be discharged only *as a body*. Consequently, the exercise of trusteeship does not lie in a list of each individual trustee's interests, expertise, or responsibilities. It lies rather in the careful crafting of strategic leadership by the board acting as a formal, official body. This leadership is expressed through *written* governing policies, for they are the board's only way of establishing what it has said as a body.

The power of trustees, therefore, is not as individuals, but as a group, a corporate entity entrusted by the public with the authority to govern and lead the organization. The only way the board can speak as the board, then, is by bringing its diverse points of view to one point. Your president does not work for several individuals, but for one board that speaks with one voice. The president cannot be held accountable when expectations are equivocal, so the board—as an agent morally big enough to embrace diversity—has an obligation to arrive at a single, unambiguous position with which, as a body, to instruct the president.

Let us take a moment to examine what this does not mean. The one-voice principle does not mean that there should be unanimity or lack of diversity on the board. On the contrary, on behalf of the ownership, the board must embrace all of the diversity it can and then reach out to obtain more. Differences among trustees are not only to be respected, but encouraged. Rarely will a vote be unanimous. Those trustees who lose the vote, however, must accept that the board has spoken and that its decision must be implemented as decided. Although dissenting board members need not pretend to *agree* with the majority decision, they must totally support—in the case of matters delegated to the president—the obligation of the president to be bound by the official board decision, not their own.

Most boards will agree that their authority is corporate rather than individual. Most will agree that the board should act in a way which is consistent with a "one-voice" approach, that the board should not present conflicting messages to its community or staff. But for beliefs to be manifest in consistent practice, boards must avoid a number of traditionally-accepted, internal mechanisms that belie the one-voice concept. Let us examine a few ways in which trustees can unintentionally dilute the commitment to speaking with one voice.

The Chair

Curiously, one effective way to destroy the one voice of the board is through board officers. Often the chair has been given a job which allows or even demands that she or he interfere with the corporate power of the board. For example, charging the chair of the board with "general oversight" of the college or "supervision" of the president places the chair between the board and the president. The chair has therefore displaced the board's one voice because the chair is then authorized to interpret to the president the wishes of the board. (In effect, the chair thereby becomes the actual CEO.) Such interpretation is unnecessary if the board has made its policies clear. Community college governance works much better if the chair is responsible to ensure that the board accomplishes its own job, rather than responsible for the performance of the president. We will discuss the chair's vital role later.

The Treasurer

Bylaws often include words suggesting that the treasurer is responsible for the books of accounts, deposits, and disbursement of monies. Actually, this work is performed under the president by accounting and finance professionals. The treasurer cannot really be held responsible for these matters without having financial staff report to him or her, thereby being able to instruct them on job performance. Boards are right to be concerned that the financial management of the college meet certain standards, but placing the treasurer between the board and the staff organization confounds delegation and disrupts the one-voice principle.

Treasurers can serve a useful purpose on the board by helping trustees with less financial experience understand the matters which will inform their policy making. The treasurer's role is never legitimate, however, if he or she is given individual authority to direct staff actions. Having a board member as treasurer is an outmoded structure of control, one completely unnecessary and potentially damaging when the board has a chief executive officer.

Committees

It is common for boards to create committees with mandates related to areas of staff responsibility. These committees are often set up in order to be instructive to staff in specified areas of college management. Personnel, building, finance, and curriculum committees are common examples of such committees. It is easy to see that such committees, set up to instruct the staff, *must* violate the one-voice principle in order to function.

The problem is less clear in the case of committees which are established by the board to be *advisory* to staff. These committees often see themselves as taking a helpful role, for it is true that staff, like everyone else, require advice at times. However, the board's prescribing the manner in which staff should obtain advice and appointing advisors overlooks that staff are adults who can obtain advice on their own when they need it. Worse, there is no way of knowing whether the board-prescribed advice is useful, since staff will either (a) refuse to trust that committee input is *really* advice or (b) pretend that the advice is helpful enough to compensate for the staff time for committee education required to get it.

Staff will, of course, accept (or pretend to accept) advice from board committees. This situation invites game playing. Much board and staff time is thus wasted by committees, which is ironic, because trustees truly wish to be helpful. The problem is not that individual trustees wish to help, but when they try to render help through an official organ of the board (a board committee), they blur the distinction between real advice and veiled instruction no matter how sterling their intent. Moreover, trustees are not helping if they merely add another component to the decision process. Boards should remember that staff spend as much time *almost* making decisions, which then must be passed through committees, as they would spend actually making the decisions. It is better to let staff know that advice from individuals is available *should staff request it*, but that the board itself will only form committees to assist the board with its job, not the staff with their job.

If trustees will merely leave staff a completely free hand in establishing any advisory mechanisms they need, the problems associated with board committees that are related to areas of staff responsibility evaporate.

The Executive Committee. Happily, many community college boards are small enough that they have never felt the need to establish executive committees. When executive committees exist, most trustees would agree that these special groups are somewhat different from other board committees, that they are "more equal" than the rest. Ordinarily this is because the executive committee has been given the right to take action between board meetings as if it were the board. In the case of boards which meet every month or every quarter, it is difficult to understand why governance action would be needed between meetings, unless the board operates with an overly short-term perspective. Further, it is usual that executive committees operate with few or no guidelines or limits on their action, and as a result become very powerful.

Placed between the board and the president, an executive committees's power must be taken from that of the board or that of the president, for there is nowhere else it can originate. Often it is from both. Executive committees therefore diminish the authority of the board and the president, greatly disrupting the board's ability to govern with one voice as well as the board's ability to hold its president accountable as a true CEO.

Appropriate Committees. In light of the discussion just above, it might seem that boards should never have committees or that board committees are never justified. That is not true, however, for there are situations in which creation of a board committee can be very helpful. Just remember that legitimacy rests primarily on one factor: A board committee can only help with a task that belongs to the board; it cannot help with a task that has been delegated away to someone else.

As to committees with which trustees are currently familiar, it is difficult to make definitive comments. It is risky to decide if a committee is appropriate based on its title alone. Legitimacy is determined by the "product" expected of the committee—whether it is a board product rather than a staff product—more than by the topic of committee activity. A finance committee is legitimate if its product is, for example, a carefully crafted set of options and implications concerning long-term reserves from which the board will make a choice. A finance committee is not legitimate if its product is advice to the president or chief financial officer on how to construct the budget.

Consequently, commenting on committees by their titles alone— trusting that everyone means the same thing by such titles—is akin to judging books by their covers. The following comments should be viewed in light of that risk.

A committee to help the board replace itself or its officers—perhaps called a recruiting committee or nominating committee—is appropriate. A committee to help the board weigh varying issues about long-term ends—perhaps called a vision committee or outcomes committee (though never a curriculum committee, which would focus on means)—is appropriate. A committee to help the board in its connections with the public—perhaps a community focus committee—is appropriate. There might be many others. Inappropriate committees—again, assuming that their titles imply what such committees normally do—are personnel, program, curriculum, grounds, and any others that deal with staff means issues.

Renegade Trustees

The principle of one voice is often broken by the individual trustee who, thinking that he or she is being helpful, goes directly to the president or those reporting to the president and instructs or meddles in staff operations. The board may not know that this is happening, since the staff has no socially acceptable way to bring such behavior to the board's attention. A board committed to governing with one voice should not wait until the renegade phenomenon becomes obvious before protecting its governance from such trustees.

The solution is rather straightforward: the board tells the president that he or she will never be answerable to trustees as individuals, and that trustees who attempt to govern as individuals may be safely ignored. Such a communication from the board to the president does not weaken, but, in fact, strengthens the power of the board as a body to instruct the president. For trustees to safeguard the wholeness of their trust, they must as a body protect staff from trustees as individuals.

PRINCIPLE 3 Board Decisions Should Predominately Be Policy Decisions

A great deal is typically said about boards' working with policy. But seldom is the term given enough definition to form a creditable foundation for modern governance. The Policy Governance model defines policy as *the value or perspective that underlies action*, but goes on to delineate strict rules as to its form.

At first, this simple definition appears to muddle the matter, since with this description it can be said that *everyone* makes *policy continually* in their occupational and personal lives. For example, the fact that you are reading these words now indicates that you made a policy (value) decision that reading this book is more valuable at this moment than doing something else.

It is obvious, then, that most policies in real life are unwritten, for persons rarely make all their values explicit, even those that determine rather momentous behaviors. Policy Governance requires boards to debate and write down their important values, and to do so in a carefully crafted way. Deciding what are "important" values and what "carefully crafted" implies would be difficult without the framing imposed by a conceptual model.

In Policy Governance, the board of trustees must address the largest or broadest values in four categories in order to fulfill this mandate.

1. ENDS Policies. These are defined as the benefits, the recipients, and the costs of those benefits intended to accrue due to operation of the college.

2. EXECUTIVE LIMITATIONS Policies. These are the guiding principles that relate to the methods or practices ("means") used by the president and staff as they accomplish the college's ENDS. For reasons to be stated later, these policies are curiously expressed in the negative, hence they act as constraints on executive authority.

3. GOVERNANCE PROCESS Policies. These are the rules that the board sets for itself with respect to the way it will perform its governing role. They also describe the board's relationship with outside interests.

4. BOARD-STAFF LINKAGE Policies. These policies describe the manner in which the board will delegate authority to the president and monitor the president's performance or, stated differently, the way governance will connect with management.

These four policy categories are designed to be exhaustive. Beyond the bylaws, there is *nothing* the board needs to say for the purposes of governing that does not fit into one of these categories. Henceforth, when referring to any one of these four policy categories, we will employ the special typographical treatment shown above. For example, "The board must routinely monitor college achievement as set forth in the board's ENDS policies." When we are referring merely to the concept and not to the actual policy category, regular typographical treatment will be used. For example, "It is critical that trustees learn to distinguish ends from means."

PRINCIPLE 4 Boards Should Formulate Policy by Determining the Broadest Values Before Progressing to More Narrow Ones

Policies may be about very important, large issues, or they may be about less important, smaller issues. A "large" policy decision will contain all smaller, related policies—a "logical containment" that omits nothing. The decision to purchase a new car is a larger decision than the decision to buy a two-door or a four-door model. Thus smaller decisions lie within larger decisions. It only makes sense to settle large issues before attempting to settle smaller ones.

Knowing that values come in sizes and that large value determinations contain ranges within which smaller ones occur is a key to the organization of board policies. If you can visualize a nested set, such as a set of mixing bowls, you can see that hands-off control of the inner bowls is assured by hands-on control of the outermost bowl. The board can establish control over large issues in the four categories, then—knowing that it is in control of the big picture—decide subsequently how much further detail it wishes to go into. The board can go into as much detail as it chooses (thereby exercising direct control of the smaller bowls) as long as it goes in one level at a time. But when it reaches a sufficient level of policy detail, it must be ready to delegate all further definition to someone else, and to accept any reasonable interpretation of its policies from that someone else. When the board performs its job appropriately, then, delegation can be defined as (a) the designation of ranges within which other persons are not only empowered to act, but are required to act and (b) the designation of who the other persons are. As we will see, to whom the board delegates will depend on the policy type.

In deciding board policies—working from broadest inward—the most painstaking board will reach a degree of detail that satisfies its need to be accountable. With respect to topics in the ENDS and EXECUTIVE LIMITATIONS categories, the board then turns subsequent interpretation over to the president. It does so because ENDS and EXECUTIVE LIMITATIONS policies are instructive about college operations. With respect to topics in the GOVERNANCE PROCESS and BOARD-STAFF LINKAGE categories, the board turns subsequent interpretation over to the chair. It does so because GOVERNANCE PROCESS and BOARD-STAFF LINKAGE policies deal with the board's own practices.

No words that the board might use can be so specific as not to require interpretation. *The only choice the board has is how great a range of subsequent interpretation is acceptable.* With respect to decisions to be made within topics covered by ENDS and EXECUTIVE LIMITATIONS policies, the board has control of the range of interpretation to be made by the president, then gets out of the way and lets the president interpret. Similarly, with respect to decisions to be made within topics covered by GOVERNANCE PROCESS and BOARD-STAFF LINKAGE policies, the board has control of the *range* of interpretation to be made by the chair, then lets the chair interpret. Of course, the president and the chair, each in his or her respective domain, have to be able to show that his or her interpretations were, in fact, reasonable interpretations of the board's words. If this "reasonable interpretation" test is passed, there can be no further evaluative judgement made by trustees of any action or decision. Indeed, if the test is passed, even the board as a whole, while it may revise its rules for the future, cannot judge past performance on criteria which it now wishes it had stated earlier.

Policy Governance, therefore, requires that the board establish policy from the broad to the more narrow in a disciplined manner. So the board addresses issues in sequence depending on size—*not* depending on the issues which an individual trustee may want on the agenda— before delegating all further definition to someone else. The board may develop policy to whatever detail it wishes as long as it does so in this orderly fashion. But all boards discover that when policy making is approached in this way, a great deal of leadership and control can be exercised without going into much detail at all.

PRINCIPLE 5 A Board Should Define and Delegate, Rather Than React and Ratify

Boards are accustomed to approving plans brought to them by staff. But there are predictable problems caused by this traditional practice. The very act of approving forces boards to become entangled in trivia. Moreover, approvals are usually issued without explicit clarification of the criteria trustees were using as they gave their approval. Further, approving staff plans causes a major problem in that it "freezes" into place detailed portions of staff plans, details which cannot then be changed without a re-approval by the board. The obstruction this constitutes for staff creativity and agility is a severe disadvantage to the college. (The impediment it places on board leadership—by having to focus on so much detail—is a severe handicap as well.) As the external and internal environments change—some daily—the president must be able to adapt and change practices. Board approval as a control device denies him or her the ability to make needed changes in an agile manner and denies trustees time for deciding the very policies that would make such role confusion unnecessary.

Staff plans are composed of decisions of various sizes about intended practices, results, students, curricula, and costs. They fall, therefore, within the board's larger policy decisions about these matters. Consequently, staff plans can be judged on their compliance with the board's ENDS and EXECUTIVE LIMITATIONS policies. Having board policies in place ahead of time allows board and staff alike to know whether a staff plan is approvable, for all the criteria by which an approval decision would be made are clear for everyone to see. When this is true, there is no reason for a staff plan to be produced that is unapprovable and, as it turns out, no reason for the board to approve staff plans at all!

The board does need to be assured that staff plans are, in fact, true to the applicable board policies. But that reassurance is best attained through a focused monitoring system wherein only the relevant criteria are checked. We will discuss monitoring a little later, but for now it can be pointed out that comparison to pre-stated criteria differs from board approval. The practice of approval lays an entire staff document in all its detail out for board perusal. What results is a kind of wandering about in a mixture of small and large issues, relevant and irrelevant ones—a spotty process that is neither informed by pre-established criteria nor, when all is said and done, results in producing any.

Notice that having criteria in place ahead of time is thoroughly compatible with the one-voice principle and even strongly reinforces it. In a normal approval procedure, however, individual trustees rely on *their own individual criteria* to decide whether to vote for or against approval. With the proactive criteria approach, trustees can no longer make individual judgments of staff plans (if they were only advisors rather than governors, they could do so). Due to the power of the governing role and the group nature of its expression, trustees can bring their individual opinions to bear only on convincing their trustee colleagues about provisions of policy itself. Such responsible, proactive behavior by a board is felt by staff as a welcome and pleasing clarity.

If we look at a budget, for example, it is clear that a vast amount of work has been invested in it by the time it reaches the board table. In other words, the preparation of your president's recommended budget consumes considerable resources—easily running into five figures, perhaps approaching six. Trustees know that a CEO-created budget could have characteristics that would keep the board from approving it. It seems only sensible, therefore, for the board to clarify those characteristics *before* the expenditure of so many resources. Once the board has stated what these characteristics are, its job is immediately transformed from approving the budget to merely ensuring that its budget policy is not violated. Remember that budget policy, like all other board policy, is created from the broadest concerns toward the narrower ones. Doing so has the effect of starting with policy that is open to a wide range of interpretation and adding to it policy language that is open to less interpretation.

PRINCIPLE 6 Ends Determination is the Pivotal Duty of Governance

The justification for any organization lies outside the organization— with its ownership—not inside the organization. A community college exists so that the world in which it operates can be a better place. Your community college does not exist for anything it is *doing*—that is, for its own activity, even the most laudable of activity. It exists for its *effects*. It exists not for teaching but for learning. The ends of an organization are the reasons for its existence. It is obvious that careful, wise selection of ends is the highest calling of trustee leadership.

The job of the community college is to achieve a socially justifiable "swap" of costs and benefits. Consider costs in a broad way: The world must give up tax money, charitable contributions, and the energy of staff and faculty whose dedication might have been used elsewhere. Consider benefits just as broadly: That same world gains citizens with skills for employment, ability to participate in civic life, and the capacity to use leisure time productively. Policies of the board of trustees included in the ENDS category deal directly with this swap of benefits for costs.

Thus, the board's ENDS policies directly answer the questions "What good will be produced for which people, at what cost?" The "good" can be expressed as a result, benefit, life change, improved circumstances, or other gain *by the consumer or affected population*. The "which people" must always be persons *outside* the operating organization, for example, students, clients, patients, communities, or segments of populations. The "cost" is any indicator of worth. It might sometimes be expressed in the way an accountant would use the word cost, perhaps in dollars, but it can always be seen in the economist's sense of "opportunity cost." In order to obtain a certain benefit for certain people, we are willing to give up sums of money, other competing results, or intangibles like public favor.

Incongruously, though answers to these questions are pivotal, ends are issues to which boards traditionally give negligible attention, if they attend to them at all. Community colleges are not alone. Virtually every organization defines itself as a provider of services of some kind or another, that is, it describes the activities engaged in by the staff as if these activities were themselves the organization's reasons for existence.

To take a rigorous ends approach is difficult, especially since it is so contrary to our traditional learning about the nature of board deliberation. In order to conceptualize ends as they relate to your college, you must focus not on activities but on outcomes. This focus demands strictness and determination in grappling with what level of accomplishment should be expected in return for expenditure. But it also requires making the tough decisions about which groups will be recipients of the benefits defined: who will be served and likely who will not be served. This means turning your attention away from budgets, personnel issues, curriculum, or buildings, and refocusing on the reasons for which the college exists at all. No college was *ever* founded in order to have a good budget...or fine personnel policies...or well kept grounds...or good parking facilities.

Even boards that devote considerable time to ENDS policies can find themselves mired down in their ends work by the difficulty of accurately measuring or evaluating ends. It is tempting to define only those ends which are easily measurable. It is better, however to thoroughly resolve ends issues and only then to address the evaluation questions. This means that discussion of evaluation should never enter board deliberation until the board has completed deciding what it wants the community college to accomplish. Even then, boards should remember the management adage that with respect to affecting organizational direction, a crude measure of the right thing beats a precise measure of the wrong thing!

Let us emphasize the importance of care in creating the board's ENDS policies. Because this kind of board deliberation constitutes such a strong break with tradition, it is easy to introduce errors that can negate its powerful advantages. Beware of the following flaws in recognizing and in defining ends work.

- *Only* those issues that *directly* address what benefit, which recipients, and what cost for the benefit are ends issues. If a decision or activity substantially affects an ends issue, it is often mistakenly treated as an ends issue itself. For example, offering a course in history would seem to affect whether students acquire a knowledge of history. Achieving a certain level of history knowledge is a legitimate ends matter, but the means to get there—even one so closely related as history curriculum—are not.

- It is common for the word "ends" to be misunderstood as meaning the endpoint in a process. For example, if we plan to have payroll records computerized by March, all the preparatory work might be considered means and the timely, completed computerization the "end." But this use of the word refers merely to an endpoint in the development of a means (computerization). Because in this usage, the word does not refer to the specification of the consumer benefit, the beneficiary, or the cost of that benefit, it does not qualify as an ends matter.

- Sometimes boards will think that any issue that is important must therefore be an ends issue. Not so. Many means issues are quite important, such as the decision to be self-insured or not. Degree of importance does not differentiate ends from means.

- If a desired state is called a goal (or, in some cases, a strategic objective), some will mistakenly assume it to be an ends issue. The language of goals and objectives can be very useful, but does not distinguish ends and means. Organizations have goals *and* objectives about ends *and* means. It is best simply to drop the words goal and objective from governance language inasmuch as they obscure the more salient distinction between ends and means.

- If a trustee is of the opinion that a certain issue should be decided by the board rather than staff, he or she will sometimes assume that this in itself makes the matter an ends issue. The person's opinion of who should decide is not a proper ends test. Moreover, not all ends decisions are made by the board anyway. Most of them are made by faculty and staff (though the board makes the largest ones).

Stick with the simple test in order to avoid all these misconstructions. It is simply this, an issues is an ends issue if—and only if—it *directly* addresses what good, for which people (not the staff or faculty), or at what cost. If not, it is not an ends issue, no matter how important, no matter who decides it, no matter how closely related it is to goals, strategies, mission, or perceived board work. Ends language is *never* about what the college will be doing; it is *always* about what will be different for others.

PRINCIPLE 7   The Board's Best Control Over Staff Means is to Limit, Not Prescribe

The distinction between ends and means, rigorously applied, will enable the board to free itself from trivia, to delegate clearly and powerfully, and to turn its attention to the large issues of ends. How does it do this? Does the board ignore means issues, and if so, is this not an abdication of its responsibility?

First, let us separate the board's own means from those of the staff. Board means relate to how the board will organize, structure, and conduct itself in order to accomplish its job. We will consider this type of means later. For now we'll concern ourselves with staff methods, practices, procedures, activities, and conduct—referring to them all as "staff means." Staff means, then, are the various arrangements and actions needed to accomplish the ENDS or to safeguard the operations that produce them. It is important to understand that budgets, curricula, personnel policies, building, equipment, and a host of other matters which traditionally consume board time are staff means issues.

Policy Governance does not require that boards ignore the very weighty issues contained in staff means decisions, but rather that boards treat staff means differently from the way in which they treat ends. Simply put, the principle is this: while boards address ends issues positively—that is, boards prescribe the ends—*boards should stay out of staff means except to state what the means shall not be.* That is, the board should speak to issues of staff means in constraining or limiting language.

At first glance, this sounds a little odd and rather negative—which troubles some trustees—for the board deals with staff means issues by producing a "don't do it" list. This action by the board is like building a fence within which freedom, creativity, and action are allowed and even encouraged. Ironically, this verbally negative language is psychologically positive because it allows a freedom, the boundaries of which need not be guessed. The collection of board statements that establishes the limits of executive authority constitutes the EXECUTIVE LIMITATIONS category of board policies.

With respect to staff means, then, the board never tells its staff how to do staff jobs. It tells the president how the staff is *not* to do its job. This will be a new experience to most boards, inasmuch as traditional governance largely ignores specification of ends, but makes much of prescribing, overseeing—or meddling in—staff means. The Policy Governance method of means constraint makes it possible to govern with fewer pages of board pronouncements, less trustee dabbling into details of implementation, and greater president accountability. Even more importantly, it frees the board to concentrate on leading the institution.

PRINCIPLE 8   A Board Must Explicitly Design Its Own Products and Process

It is in the policy category of GOVERNANCE PROCESS that the board states what it expects of itself. This important category of board policy deals with a portion of the board's own means: how the board will conduct itself and perform its own job.

Boards rarely enunciate and hold fast to the principles guiding their own operation, making themselves appear directionless and even at times capricious. Under Policy Governance, the board addresses itself directly to matters which conventional governance leaves unstated: Just who does the board represent and how will it maintain contact with this constituency? What are the products which the board itself exists to produce (apart from what the college produces)? How will the board define the job of the chair, and how does it delegate to the chair? Under what circumstances will the board use committees? GOVERNANCE PROCESS policies answer these questions.

In GOVERNANCE PROCESS policies, the board commits itself to use committees only when they are necessary to help the board get its job done, but never to help the staff with their jobs. In GOVERNANCE PROCESS policies, the board delegates to the chair the right to make any reasonable interpretation of the board's words in both GOVERNANCE PROCESS and BOARD-STAFF LINKAGE policy areas. (The president will be given a parallel authority with respect to topics governed by ENDS and EXECUTIVE LIMITATIONS policies.) This delegation pattern ensures that the chair and the president work closely together, but that neither reports to the other.

It is also under GOVERNANCE PROCESS that the board outlines its own code of conduct, the way it will control and plan its own agenda, and the nature of its linkage with the community.

PRINCIPLE 9 A Board Must Forge a Linkage With Management That Is Both Empowering and Safe

Community college boards typically desire and fear a strong president. They need a strong president and an empowered staff to have a high achieving institution. However, they fear a president or staff dominant enough to steer and, at times, even ignore the board. Indeed, the seesaw of power between a board and its president is a classic phenomenon of college governance.

It is not uncommon for a board to delegate too little authority, cheating itself of the executive effectiveness the mission deserves. On the other hand, it is also not uncommon for a board to delegate too much authority, so as to abdicate its own responsibility for leadership. Thus a community college board must carefully craft a form of delegation that balances these critical ingredients.

Boards using the Policy Governance model achieve this balance by following the previously discussed principles associated with the ends-means distinction and the progression from large to smaller values. These boards set forth their style of delegation in the BOARD-STAFF LINKAGE category of policies. Viewed in another light, these policies describe the way governance and management are connected.

In the BOARD-STAFF LINKAGE category, one policy commits the board to treat its president as the chief executive officer, delegating to the staff organization in no other way but through this position. Another policy outlines the job products (that is, the values added) of the president. Yet another policy outlines how evaluation of the president's performance will take place. Incidentally, the job products of the president are rather simple to define and evaluate: The president is responsible to ensure that the organization as a whole (a) accomplishes expectations as set out by the board in its ENDS policies and (b) does not engage in the means which the board has prohibited in its EXECUTIVE LIMITATIONS policies.

PRINCIPLE 10 Performance of the President Must Be Monitored Rigorously, But Only Against Policy Criteria

When the board has told its president to achieve certain ends without violating certain EXECUTIVE LIMITATIONS, monitoring performance becomes no less—and no more—than checking actual performance against these two sets of expectations.

In Policy Governance, monitoring is only against existing board-stated criteria in the ENDS and EXECUTIVE LIMITATIONS policies. The board may establish whatever criteria it wishes in those policies, but it cannot monitor criteria it *meant* to establish but did not. Having set the criteria, it must demand information that directly addresses these criteria. For example, the board which has outlined its "don't do it" list with respect to the college's financial condition cannot accept a balance sheet or income statement as financial monitoring. They may be informative reports, but information precisely targeted to the relevant criteria is either not available in such documents or is hard to find.

Following this rule, the board can assure receiving relevant monitoring data without having to digest enormous amounts of unnecessary information. It will become obvious that traditional attempts at monitoring—the methods so familiar to us all—are more an exercise in foraging about than rigorous inspection to see if criteria were met. (Information required by the board to assist it in its decision making is of a different variety, and should not be confused with monitoring information or the principles that apply to it.) Hence, information for monitoring is targeted and precise, always directly addressing criteria set by the board.

CHAPTER 2

Describing the Board's Job

Building on the foregoing principles, we can summarize the job of the board. Policy Governance requires the board's job description, just like the president's job description, to be presented not as a list of activities, but as a statement of "values added" or, if you will, job products. The board's job description consists of a list of at least three outputs:

1. *Linkage with the Ownership:* The board provides the only legitimate bridge between those who morally own the college (for a community college, probably the general public of a community, region, or state) and the operating organization.

2. *Written Governing Policies:* Using principles addressed earlier, the board establishes the largest values of the organization in the categories of ENDS, EXECUTIVE LIMITATIONS, GOVERNANCE PROCESS, and BOARD-STAFF LINKAGE.

3. *Assurance of Executive Performance:* The board does not *do* the community college's work, but it must *assure* that it is done.

You will notice that the foregoing is not a list of staff-like jobs, but are "values added," clearly distinguishable from products of management. These three outputs are the minimum, non-delegable outputs to be produced by the board. A board can decide to add job outputs to this list, but cannot delete any of them. For example, a given community college board might add the achievement of an endowment or of a particular legislative change to its job description. It is best to add outputs sparingly, since there is always the risk of diluting the original, critical three.

You will also notice that the board's job outputs are *always means* as opposed to ends. This should not be surprising inasmuch as the community college does not exist to have good governance. Good governance exists to describe and assure a good community college. While it is the staff and faculty's job to *create* the outputs of a good community college, it is the board's job to *define* them, at least at the broad level of description.

The Agenda

To most trustees, the concrete embodiment of the board's job is the agenda for a specific board meeting. The agenda can be seen as a one-meeting "piece" of the longer-term job to be done by the board. In other words, the board's job description is the basis for decisions about the content of meeting agendas. Operating with a clearer picture of its job, the board is able to develop its own agenda based on the job it is to accomplish. Notice that this means that the board agenda is *the board's* agenda, not the president's agenda for the board.

Meeting agendas should not be created one meeting at a time. The board cannot effectively take control of its agendas if it only collects trustees' ideas at the end of one meeting about the next. Agendas must emerge as short-term tasks founded in a longer-term process. What follows is a way for boards to create meeting agendas.

Consider the job description shown above as the board's *perpetual agenda*, from which annual and, in turn, single meeting agendas are to be derived. According to principles covered earlier, the chair is normally authorized to fill in details of the board's broad-brush determination of anything in the GOVERNANCE PROCESS topics, including the board agenda. Hence, the agenda of any given meeting would likely be produced by the chair. But it would be based on the broader statements recorded by the board in an applicable GOVERNANCE PROCESS policy, perhaps one in which the board has sketched an annual board work plan, or perhaps in a policy entitled "Agenda Control."

Since the board meeting is the main device used by the board to get its job done, any meeting can only reflect some part of the job the board has assigned itself. We have established in this chapter that the board's job is to produce at least three outputs: (1) a creditable linkage with the ownership, (2) governing policies of four sorts, (3) an assurance of the president's performance, and any other outputs the board has formally accepted as its own responsibility.

The board meeting, therefore, will be a forum in which work on some part of these board outputs takes place. We are not concerned with the traditional divisions of agenda work into old business, new business, and committee reports. As you can see, these divisions bear no relation to the governance model or to the board outputs. We encourage boards to divide their meeting agendas in a way that both reflects and reinforces the reasons for meeting in the first place! While doing so offers a multitude of concrete agenda forms, let's look at some characteristics the resulting agendas are likely to have.

Some aspects of linking with the ownership and work on ENDS policies will probably show up on every agenda. These two tasks are never ending; they are properly subjects of continual board obsession rather than of sporadic attention.

With respect to the linking process, trustee time will be spend on discussing and planning the linkages as well as on actually carrying them out. Hence, at least some board agendas will have nothing to do with meeting around the college board table, but with observing and meeting with other boards and other natural community groups. With respect to ENDS, the board will need to spend a high percentage of available trustee time exploring, gathering wisdom, debating and deciding ENDS provisions that are thoroughly grounded in community input, hard data, and strategic vision.

The board's trusteeship role *vis-a-vis* the community requires that the board continually revisit its mechanisms for obtaining input from the community, and that it formulate its ENDS using that input as well as new information on the changing external environment. Gathering community input is not an easy task, so boards should be as creative as possible in structuring input systems. Focus groups, surveys, board-to-board discussions, trustee "ambassadors" to natural groupings (churches, neighborhoods), and a host of other possibilities should be tested. Remember, the input the board is seeking is input about ends, not about staff means.

Further, although consuming less time than the foregoing items, assurance of executive performance will also show up on almost every agenda. Because regular monitoring reports that are mailed to trustees will achieve most of that assurance, there is normally no need to make such reports part of the board meeting. What can profitably be on the agenda, however, is trustee discussion about whether the reports provide adequate assurance. Are they understandable? Do they convincingly provide data reasonably related to the policy-stated criteria? In other words, whether the monitoring system is working is a frequent agenda item, but not the monitoring information itself, unless reports or other sources suggest that criteria are *not* being met.

Work on developing or updating GOVERNANCE PROCESS, BOARD-STAFF LINKAGE, and EXECUTIVE LIMITATIONS policies will probably not show up on every agenda after the board has passed the start-up period of getting policies initially in place. Policies in these categories do occasionally require amendment, but their relative stability causes them to be only infrequently in need of change.

We cannot comment on the optional board outputs (like reaching a particular level of endowment or change in legislation), for boards would vary so widely with respect to the optional portion of their job descriptions. Suffice it to say, however, that if the board has seen fit to assume responsibility for a job output, the board must provide time to achieve it.

As you might expect, a more sophisticated leadership role for the college board will compel a more rigorous approach to self-evaluation. The board will have to monitor its own performance far more compulsively than it monitors staff performance, for the tendency for a group process to stray is overwhelming. We recommend not an annual evaluation, but an evaluation of board process no less than once per meeting. Therefore, a regular spot on the agenda is reserved for evaluation of the board itself.

In self-evaluation, the board refers to its rules for itself. Against these criteria it judges its performance. Notice that board self-evaluation ceases to be a matter of whether individual trustees feel connected or validated, but focuses rather on whether the board's products and processes are those committed to in the applicable board policies.

The ongoing evaluation need not be an onerous task. Perhaps it is merely a short discussion comparing real board activity and performance to one or more of the GOVERNANCE PROCESS or BOARD-STAFF LINKAGE policies in which the board has set forth expectations for its own behavior.

So when a board uses the Policy Governance model, its meetings take on a new appearance. There will be virtually no trivial matters at the board table and no "approvals" of staff and faculty plans. There is very little inspection of last month or last quarter since monitoring will have been made straightforward enough that it occurs in intelligible, largely mailed reports. Boards no longer deal with lists of staff issues, but rather spend their time receiving information and education which will equip them to make long-term ends decisions in the best interests of the community. They reach out for input from the community and from other boards which represent the community in other endeavors. Boards behave, in short, in a manner which demonstrates that their allegiance is an external, community-focused one. In a trustee capacity, they become not supermanagers of the college apparatus, but leaders and builders of the future.

As compared with board meetings under traditional governance, then, Policy Governance board meetings will tend toward the following description:

- Fewer items are on the agenda, though more important ones and ones of longer term nature.
- Ends issues dominate the agenda in terms of deliberation and decision making, along with the community linkage and other trustee education needed to wisely consider them.
- Monitoring college performance—particularly the monitoring of EXECUTIVE LIMITATIONS criteria—is largely by mail rather than at meetings.
- Monitoring college performance on ENDS is by mail mostly, but occasionally on the agenda to stimulate further ENDS exploration and development.

- Many "meetings" are not meetings at all, but excursions and co-meetings with other boards, community groups, elected officials, and others.

It is with some hesitation that we offer the example of a board agenda shown in this chapter, since we do not want the example to be seen as a model boards should follow. Our example is true to the principles of Policy Governance, of course, but there are innumerable other agenda styles that, though differing from ours in both format and content, would nonetheless be consistent with the principles.

Board meetings created in this way are a true reflection of the job description. That is, the community college board will be continually engaged in the big issues that befit leaders. Or, more accurately, the board will be engaged in *leading leaders*—for as surely as the board must lead, it must do so in a way that optimizes the leadership of its president, its staff, and its faculty.

HAPPY VALLEY COMMUNITY COLLEGE
BOARD OF TRUSTEES

Notice of Meeting
October 18, 1994
9:00 a.m. to 3:00 p.m.

AGENDA

1. CALL TO ORDER

2. MINUTES APPROVAL: September Board Meeting

3. MONITORING CONFIRMATION

   [Each trustee affirms having read and understood all monitoring reports received since the September meeting.]

4. OWNERSHIP LINKAGE

   Discussion of options paper produced by board Outreach Committee investigating community focus group methods. Decision on trial strategy.

   [amends board policy "Community Input"]

5. ENDS

   Presentation by CEO, Happy Valley Chamber of Commerce, "Community Employment Trends and Future Employment Needs," followed by discussion.

   [part of board education leading to ENDS decisions to be made in March]

6. EXECUTIVE LIMITATIONS

   Motion to reduce specificity of board policy "Asset Protection" by removing definition of "material."

7. INCIDENTAL INFORMATION

   a. Upcoming concert in Lecture Hall 2

   b. Football standings

8. BOARD EVALUATION

   Trustees Brown and Smith will provide a comparison of board meeting content and conduct to board policies "Governing Style," "Agenda Control," and "Delegation to the President."

9. ADJOURNMENT

CHAPTER 3

A Trustee's Approach to the Job

One of the reasons that a trustee's job is so difficult is that "the job" is essentially a group responsibility. In fact, it is hard to discuss how an individual is to approach a group task. Yet each trustee has a responsibility to come with an effective mind set, to carry out his or her part of preparation and participation, and to take responsibility for the group. These are not always easy tasks.

Some advice follows on the frame of mind and individual preparations necessary for a given trustee to play an effective role in creating a productive board.

Be prepared to participate responsibly. Participating responsibly means to do your homework, to come prepared to work (sometimes the work is listening), to agree and disagree as your values dictate, and to accept the group decision as legitimate even if not—in your opinion—correct. It is not acceptable, for example, to have opinions but not express them.

Remember your identity is with the community, not the staff. Identifying closely with your staff will be inviting, in that you may be in conversation with them about community college issues more than with members of the public. You will come to use their abbreviations and short-hand language. Be careful that you don't become more connected with staff than with those who own the college. Be a microcosm of the public, not a shadow of the staff.

Represent the ownership, not a single constituency. You will understand and personally identify with one or more constituencies more than others. That provincial streak is natural in everyone, but your civic trusteeship obligation is to rise above it. If you are a teacher, you are not on the board to represent teachers. If you are a private businessperson, you are not there to represent that interest. If you are a student, you are not there to represent the interest of today's students. You are a trustee for the broad ownership, the public. There is no way the board can be big enough to have a spokesperson for every legitimate interest, so in a moral sense you must stand for them all. Think of yourself as being from a constituency, but not representing it.

Be responsible for group behavior and productivity. While doing your own job as a single trustee is important, it does not complete your responsibility. You must shoulder the potentially unfamiliar burden of being responsible for the group. That is, if you are part of a group that doesn't get its job done, that meddles in administration, or that breaks it own rules, you are culpable.

Be a proactive trustee. You are not a trustee to hear reports. You are a trustee to make governance decisions. Listening while staff or committees recount what they have been busy doing is boring and unnecessary. Of course, it is sometimes important to get data through reports, but don't let that cast you in a passive role. Even when you are receiving education, do so as an active participant, searching doggedly for the wisdom that will enable good board decisions.

Honor divergent opinions without being intimidated by them. You are obligated to register your honest opinion on issues the board takes up, but other trustees are obligated to speak up as well. Encourage your colleagues to express their opinions without allowing your own to be submerged by louder or more insistent comrades. You are of little use to the process if full expression of your ideas can be held hostage.

Use your special expertise to inform your colleagues' wisdom. If you work in accounting, law, construction, or another skilled field, be careful not to take your colleagues off the hook with respect to board decisions about such matters. To illustrate, an accountant trustee shouldn't assume personal responsibility for assuring fiscal soundness. But it is all right for him or her to help trustees understand what fiscal jeopardy looks like or what indices of fiscal health to watch carefully. With that knowledge, the board can pool its human values about risk, brinkmanship, over-extension, and so forth in the creation of fiscal policies. In other words, use your special understanding to inform the board's wisdom, but never to substitute for it.

Orient to the whole, not the parts. Train yourself to examine, question, and define the big picture. Even if your expertise and comfort lie in some subpart of the community college challenge, the subpart is not your job as a trustee. You may offer your individual expertise to the president, should he or she wish to use it. But in such a role, accept that you are being a volunteer consultant and leave your trustee hat at home.

Think upward and outward more than downward and inward. There will be great temptation to focus on what goes on with administrators, staff, and faculty instead of what difference the college should make in the larger world. The latter is a daunting task for which no one feels really qualified, yet it is the trustee's job to do.

Tolerate issues that cannot be quickly settled. Shorter-term, more concrete matters can give you a feeling of completion, but are likely to involve you in the wrong issues. If you must deal with such matters, resign from the board and apply for a staff position.

But don't tolerate putting off the big issues forever. The really big issues will often be too intimidating for you to reach a solution comfortably. Yet in most cases, the decision is being made anyway by default. Board inaction itself is a decision. Don't tolerate the making of big decisions by the timid action of not making them.

Support the board's final choice. No matter which way you voted, you are obligated to support the board's choice. This obligation doesn't mean you must pretend to agree with that choice; you may certainly maintain the integrity of your dissent even after the vote. What you must support is the legitimacy of the choice that you still don't agree with. For example, you will support without reservation that the president must follow the formal board decision, not yours.

Don't mistake form for substance. Don't confuse having a PR committee with having good PR. Don't confuse having financial reports with having sound finances. Don't confuse having a president with having a CEO. Don't confuse having a token constituent board member with having sufficient input. Traditional governance has often defined responsible behavior procedurally (do this, review that, follow this set of steps) instead of substantively, so beware the trap.

Obsess about ENDS. Keep the conversation about benefits, beneficiaries, and costs of the benefits alive at all times. Converse with staff, colleague trustees, and the public about these matters. Ask questions, consider options, and otherwise fill most of your trustee consciousness with issues of ends.

Don't expect agendas to be built on your interests. The board's agenda is a product of careful crafting of the board's job, not a laundry list of trustee interests. Remember too, that you are not on the board to help the staff with your special expertise, but to govern. No matter how well you can do a staff job, as a trustee you are not there to do it or even to advise on it. If you wish to offer your help as an individual—apart from your trustee duties—do so, but take great care that all parties know you are not acting as a trustee.

The college is not there for you. Being an owner representative is very different from seeing the college as your personal possession. Remember that the college does not exist to satisfy trustees' needs to feel useful, self-actualized, involved, or entertained. Of course, it's fine to feel these things and perfectly acceptable to seek whatever fulfillment governance can give you. But the board job must be designed foremost around the right of the community to be faithfully served in the determination of what the institution should accomplish for students.

Squelch your individual points of view during monitoring. Your own values count when the board is creating policies. But when the president's performance is monitored, you must refer only to the criteria the board decided, not what your opinion was about those criteria. In other words, the president is accountable to comply with the board's decisions, but in fairness cannot be judged against yours. You should present any opinion you may have about amending the policies, of course, but not so as to contaminate the monitoring process.

Support the chair in board discipline. Although the board as a whole is responsible for its own discipline, it will have charged the chair with a special role in the group's confronting its own process. Don't make the chair's job harder, rather ask what you can do to make it easier.

Putting the New Governance Into Practice

In the previous section we examined some of the ways in which Policy Governance can assist community college trustees to address the important issues, to govern through policy, and to do so in a way that contributes to everyone's ability to perform their role with authority and flexibility.

We defined "policy" as *the value or perspective that underlies action* and described the useful distinction that boards can make between ends and means. Boards must make policies about ENDS, board means (divided into the two categories called GOVERNANCE PROCESS and BOARD-STAFF LINKAGE), and staff means (constrained by EXECUTIVE LIMITATIONS). It is important to remember that, beyond bylaws, *everything* a board says falls into one of these categories.

In other words, the board does not have policies *plus* a budget, long-range plan, personnel manual, and other such documents. Policies drafted under Policy Governance contain *all* the board's decisions and values about matters governing the college. It may at first seem hard to believe that everything a board may decide to make a policy about can be classified in one of these categories. Some practice will convince you that it is so.

Because all the official board wisdom is concentrated in this small number of carefully constructed, succinct policies, the board's policy registry is a high-leverage, powerful document that must be kept central to every board endeavor. The policies constitute a truly living document, probably from 20 to 40 pages, that is amended as frequently as necessary to be absolutely certain that it reflects current values of the board. If policies are not kept up to date, they cease to be the authoritative repository of board values and, consequently, lose their fidelity and centrality to both governance and executive management. The board policy register is the sourcebook of governance, present in every board meeting and consulted before and during any board discussion.

Drafting Explicit Board Policies

The actual policy documents are structured by size, starting with the largest issues and "moving in" to smaller ones. Hence, in a physical way the policy architecture reflects the board's moving from greater to lesser abstractions in a physical way. This progression of board decision making as well as board policy construction from broad to narrow issues is critical. Let us present the idea in graphic form before describing some of the policies a board might have.

We'll begin with a normal event in our lives, buying a personal vehicle. "A personal vehicle" in that last sentence had meaning for you even though it is a rather broad designation, open to a great deal of interpretation. We will represent the range of possible interpretation as a very wide box, a "container" capable of holding all the ways one could reasonably interpret "a personal vehicle."

This box—or this range of reasonable interpretation—is wide enough to include bicycle, car, van, truck, or motorcycle. Any one of these would be a reasonable interpretation of "a personal vehicle."

Let us be a little more specific, then, by saying that we want to acquire an automobile. Even though the range of interpretation is now much smaller (represented by a smaller box placed within the original, wider one), the word "automobile" is still open to some range of interpretation. For example, a car that is new, used, luxury, or convertible would each be a reasonable interpretation.

Let's give our intentions greater definition by saying that we want a red car. That certainly reduces the range of interpretation remaining, but by no means is there no interpretative range left.

Now, let us skip away from words to the actual behavior of choosing a car. It turns out, say, that the car we buy is red, four-door, medium-priced, two-year-old used, air conditioned. The descriptive list can go on and on, even to the small dent in the left rear fender! The actual car purchased is true to a reasonable interpretation of the increasingly finer definition mentioned above, but it is surely not the only reasonable interpretation of that definition.

What a tedious example! Why should anyone go through all these steps, when just going out and buying the car tells the story in exact detail with no bother about these decreasing "ranges of meaning"? *As an individual* I can, in fact, go do the job myself. I can purchase the car without all the fuss we are recommending for boards. But if we are managing other people...and if we want them to be able to use their own judgment and creativity (after all, we're paying for it), then we cannot make all the determinations and carry out the actual behaviors. This is true for every supervisor with a few workers, but for a part-time board governing the work of scores or hundreds of staff and faculty, it is absolutely crucial.

A community college board of trustees is faced with a job so large that does not have the option to do the job itself. Yet it is accountable for *all* activities, decisions, states of being, and achievement of the entire college. The board has only three options with which to approach such overwhelming accountability:

1. The board can (a) fail to state the larger values within which staff must operate, thereby (b) leaving them to guess what the board wants, (c) then poke, probe, oversee, examine, and assess staff plans and behaviors—in effect, judging staff on criteria the board never stated. This practice is the commonly accepted approval syndrome of board control.

2. The board can (a) fail to state the larger values within which staff must operate, (b) but allow the staff to make decisions as it wishes. This is the widely prevalent, though not commonly accepted, practice called rubber stamping.

3. The board can (a) state the larger values, coming into greater detail as far as it chooses, (b) allow staff to make *any* decisions that are reasonable interpretations of the board's greatest detail, and (c) require monitoring data to disclose that plans and actions have truly been within the criteria the board stated.

Obviously, it is route number 3 that we urge community college boards to adopt. But governance tradition is such that college boards have inherited a predominant use of modes 1 and 2.

What's the Catch?

The prescription we give here is as *simple* as it appears, though fulfilling the challenge is not necessarily *easy*. There are some side effects and costs, however, that a board would do well to consider at the front end:

- This method requires trustees to iron out their differences in a very *explicit* way. The first challenge of explicitness involves a commitment to enunciate and to honor the diverse viewpoints trustees bring to the discussion. It is easy for the dynamics of boardroom politics or even boardroom politeness to result in squelching healthy dissent—even when no one wishes to have that effect. A strong or opinionated chair, or perhaps a board leader who is either highly respected (or just louder than most!), can damage the full expression of diversity. The board as a whole must take responsibility for using a system that makes this damage unlikely or impossible.

- The second challenge of being explicit involves a commitment to bring whatever diversity there is to a point of resolution, that is, to a decision. In other words, the board's commitment to explicit statement of its values includes strict attention both to diversity and to decisiveness. The commitment to solidarity means that the board issues only one position, not a laundry list of its various individual positions. This takes much discussion, fair play, and an intention to act as a body.

- Trustees who dissented before the vote was taken must resist the temptation to undermine the board's collective decision. A great deal of time and effort is spent by boards that bring diversity to resolution. Undermining that resolution once reached wastes trustees' commitment and muddies delegation to the president.

- The method requires trustees to settle their differences *one level at a time*, just as if they were components in a nested set. This level-at-a-time approach takes discipline while policy is being developed, to be sure, but pays great dividends in time saved later.

Remember that trustees are deliberating and generating *their own values* in this process, not reacting to a staff or committee recommendation. Because of this, trustees will not have before them a complete document that they are picking through. They may have several very broadly phrased alternative statements in each category of issues. It is acceptable for a committee of the board or other source to have assembled several such statements as long as they cover an unbiased breadth of possibilities. It is   acceptable for another group to sift through the possibilities and select one to recommend to the board, even if such practice is the generally accepted mode of committee operation.

It is important that the board debate the options and finally adopt some statement that best arises out of trustees' values. Having done so, trustees can then go on to discuss and determine sub-issues, that is, issues at a more detailed level—tantamount to moving to the next smaller box in our nested set example.

- This method requires trustees to stand behind the words they have chosen to use. The commitment to own its own words extends both to the board's relationship with the president and to the board's relationship with the public. Since governance is a verbal job, saying what you mean and meaning what you say must be a credo.

- This method requires trustees to let—even require—others to make decisions. In other words, empowerment of other people is not an option, but a necessity of good community college governance.

- This method requires trustees to see themselves first and foremost as creators of the future, not reviewers of the past. Trusteeship must be more about the world trustees seek to create than merely about being carried along on the momentum of present management.

Trustees would do well to ponder the difficulties of the foregoing list. Boards should openly discuss the difficulties and strategies for overcoming them. Such strategies would be recorded in the GOVERNANCE PROCESS policy category.

Responsible and powerful governance should not be tedious, laden with trivia or ritual, but it is difficult. There is, however, a handsome payoff. When a community college board practices the kind of governance we have described, it may expect that:

- board values become much clearer and more stable
- board accountability for college values is comprehensive
- board agendas are less trivial
- the board is able to empower staff more powerfully
- the board remains clearly in control
- the board has more time for addressing the long-term vision
- the board has more time to spend on its relationship with the community, including dialogue with other boards, and with the larger social and public policy issues.

Although the Policy Governance model consists of philosophy, process, and principles about board leadership and the board-management relationship, its concrete manifestation is in carefully crafted board policies. Of course, given the significant difference between Policy Governance and the various forms of conventional board practice, "policy" means something entirely different from the definition with which boards are accustomed...and the actual documents look different.

In Chapter 5 through Chapter 8, we will examine what these policies look like. A list of policy titles will be shown for each policy category, but you are cautioned that this list is not necessarily exhaustive. Remember that all board policy making begins with the broadest statement within each of the board policy categories. Just what are the broadest statements which boards make in the four policy categories? We will proceed to examine examples of the largest or "mega" policies in each category. The wording which will be shown has been demonstrated to be helpful to boards, but it is offered only as an illustration, not as a recommendation that would be appropriate for all boards. Remember, the policies which a board puts into place are its own policies, reflecting the values and perspectives of the board. So no policy wording reproduced here can presume to be best for a particular board.

CHAPTER 5

Spotlight on the Mission: Policies of the ENDS Category

Without any doubt, the ENDS category of board policy is the most challenging to boards of trustees, and the most demanding of their time, talents, and energies.

You will recall that ends directly address the specific questions: "What good? For which people? At what cost?" Ends are long-term in perspective, and they are about who will be benefitted by the college, in what ways, and at what relative cost or opportunity cost. Policies in the other three sections can be rapidly formulated, but ENDS policies are slow to develop. Colleges (and other nonprofit and public organizations) are accustomed to describing themselves in terms of the activities of faculty and staff. Thus it is easy to make the mistake of describing programs and services, courses and curricula as ENDS, when in fact these are some of the means which we might expect to lead to the accomplishment of the board's ENDS policies.

This book cannot specify the ENDS policies of your college, as these are determined uniquely by each individual board. It will, however, offer some examples of "mega-ENDS" statements in order to illustrate the difference between ENDS statements and the words often contained in mission statements.

ENDS policies are developed by the board on behalf of the ownership of the college. Consultation with that ownership is therefore crucial. When a board has obtained a wide range of input, and has discussed the various competing values, it may start to draft a "mega" level to begin its ENDS policies.

Here are some hints which may be helpful in the process and which may help avoid the tendency to regress back into being means oriented: Avoid verbs; they encourage the board to focus on what the organization is doing rather than on the ways in which recipients will be benefitted. Use nouns: they make it more likely that the board will be precise about describing outcome conditions. Keep mega-ENDS statements very short; remember, they can be further defined in subsequent ENDS policies. Finally, think of the board as the public's purchasing agent. You are deciding what money and effort should buy—not in terms of busyness, but in terms of change for communities or students.

Starting, then, as in all other policy making, with the largest statement, the board would debate and adopt the college mission phrased in ends terminology. A mega-ENDS statement for a community college might be:

> *LaFond College exists in order that community members have the skills and knowledge sufficient for successful employment or higher education achievement.*

There are innumerable alternative ways in which this largest of ENDS statements might be drafted. Another board might have come up with "job-readiness," or perhaps "vocational and recreational alternatives," "postsecondary knowledge and skills of their choice," or some other statement. These examples grow out of different values and philosophies about education, different assessments of the need, and vary in the amount of ambition they express.

But they are all statements of *outcomes*. At this broad level, there is little specificity in the terms. The example highlighted does not clarify which vocational and academic alternatives are offered, but it does convey a commendable level of ambition. "Job-readiness" does not specify the types of jobs for which graduates will be ready. "Vocational and recreational alternatives" does not define whether the college will simply increase the alternatives available (a change in the environment) or will equip students for successful use of opportunities that exist. "Postsecondary knowledge and skills of their choice" promises that citizens will have skills and knowledge, but that the students, not the college, will choose which they will be. None of the options define which community members have priority.

It is perfectly acceptable that these statements are broad and vaguely defined. Even at this level of breadth, you can see that fervent opinions about them deserve to be aired and debated. Choosing one rather than another can result in a completely different set of further determinations needing to be made. In the option we highlighted, the board will probably elect to further define which skills and knowledge. In the third alternative, the board would not do that at all, but would further define what constitutes "of their choice." For example, does "of their choice" mean the individual choice of each student or the majority of students? The former might prescribe an impossible task for the president, while the latter can be accomplished. Of course, the board doesn't have to further define anything. It could leave all further interpretation to the president.

But boards invariably do elect to go into greater detail in defining the college's ENDS before they are comfortable leaving all further interpretation to the president. The details to be fleshed out will vary substantially from board to board, inasmuch as values among trustees and among whole boards of trustees on ends issues show great diversity. In fact, it is testimony to the wide variety of community college roles in society that ENDS policies will show greater variation from college to college than any other category of board policies. That variation will occur in the content of individual policies, to be sure, but also even in the topics boards choose to expand upon, that is, the policy titles themselves. With the risk of doing a disservice to this diversity, here is a list of policies a college board *might* have in its ENDS section:

• Vocational Priorities	...the relative priority among the production of various vocational skills;
• Recreational Priorities	...the relative priority among the various leisure time capabilities that might be engendered;
• Recipient Priorities	...the relative priority among various possible student or recipient groups;

• Academic Priorities   …the relative priorities among the various understandings and knowledge that might be produced.

It is more difficult for us to cite a sample list of ENDS policies than for the other policy categories. GOVERNANCE PROCESS and BOARD-STAFF LINKAGE will bear close resemblance among boards using the Policy Governance model simply because these categories contain many of the fundamental principles of Policy Governance. EXECUTIVVE LIMITATIONS policies tap board members' sense of prudence and ethics, values that tend toward a sameness when responsible persons get around to putting them on paper. (They vary more when left undebated, unstated, and therefore represented only in unexamined behavior.) At any rate, for these reasons we are less helpful in suggesting sample ENDS policies than for the policy categories to follow in subsequent chapters.

That said, however, we will illustrate two ENDS policies a community college board might have.

POLICY OF THE BOARD OF TRUSTEES

TITLE: Purpose	TYPE: Ends
POLICY NO: 1.1	This policy adopted on
	_____ March 1 _____ , 1995.
EFFECTIVE DATE: April 17, 1995	_____
	Secretary

LaFond College exists in order that community members have the skills and knowledge sufficient for successful employment or higher education achievement.

1. Students will be persons of any age who have a high school diploma or who, as adults, desire to attain high school diploma equivalency.

2. Students prepared for advanced academic success will have the ability and the prerequisite academic experience sufficient for entry into a four-year college or university program. This part of the college mission will constitute a substantial, though not dominant priority.

3. Students prepared for employment success will have the knowledge of occupational choices, skills, work habits, and job leads necessary for an economically self-sufficient life in the workplace. This part of the college mission will be the dominant priority.

4. Productivity in attaining these results will be at least the state of the art for community college effectiveness.

Commentary on the Board Policy *Purpose*

The previous page shows a policy in the ENDS category titled *Purpose*. This category is where the board establishes the results, recipients of the results, and acceptable costs of those results for the entire college endeavor. Stated another way, the board defines in this category what the public—in choosing to have a community college—expects to buy and for whom.

Remember that in each category of policies, the board creates the very broadest policy first, then augments it with more detailed policies. Moving in this sequence has the effect of giving increasing definition—that is, more detail—to what the board values and how it looks at things. Here the broadest statement in this category shows up as the preamble of what might be considered to be the board's master ENDS policy. The board has chosen to title the entire policy *Purpose*, though the mega-statement in the preamble would certainly fulfill the role of a mission statement.

ENDS as stated by the board are intended to be achieved. To that extent, they are not blue-sky, rhetorical musings. This policy does not begin with references to "quality of life" or "preparation for life." It starts with what aspect of life quality or preparation the college chooses to create (admitting, as it were, that it is not taking on the whole range of these larger life issues).

Nothing in this policy addresses what the college will be doing to accomplish the results for the cited recipients at the cost or efficiency noted. It is critical to leave all references to means out of ENDS policies. ENDS policies are never about methods, practices, efforts, education philosophy, or beliefs. In short, policies like this one are not about your organizational processes, but describe student or community change. They are the standards—even broadly stated—against which you will later assess your institution's effectiveness.

The preamble is given greater definition by the four numbered sections. Consider some of the board's choice of words: "substantial, though not dominant priority" in section 2 and "state of the art for community college effectiveness" in section 4. These terms clearly bias the acceptable interpretation range in an obvious direction, though the board has chosen not to pin its meaning down any more than this. Maybe this is exactly what all trustees meant, or perhaps it was a compromise between opposing alternatives. In any event, these words are the ones the president—and the board—must live with unless they are subsequently amended. The president must interpret whether colleges to which to compare LaFond are ones within the region or ones of similar size or similar student body composition. Remember that any reasonable interpretation will be acceptable. If that is not true, then the board needs to say more either in this policy or in a follow-up policy like the one we will demonstrate next.

The same comment is true for defining which occupational areas, what is self-sufficiency, which four-year colleges and universities, and so on. In each case, the board can determine further definition (as it does about academic results in the next example) or it can stop and leave interpretation to the president.

POLICY OF THE BOARD OF TRUSTEES

TITLE: Academic Results	**TYPE:** Ends
POLICY NO: 1.2	This policy adopted on
	<u> March 1 </u>, 1995.
EFFECTIVE DATE: April 17, 1995	<u> </u>
	Secretary

Academic results with students will be the ability and the prerequisite academic experience sufficient for entry into a four-year college or university program.

1. Academic abilities will emphasize broad liberal arts understandings and foundations for further achievement.
2. Entry to four-year college or university programs means, by 1997, the unqualified acceptance at a third-year level of study.
3. College or university entry requirements to be met are all public four-year colleges and universities in this state and, by 1998, at least 75 percent of private four-year colleges and universities.

Commentary on the Board Policy *Academic Results*

The facing page shows a policy in the ENDS category titled *Academic Results*. This category is where the board establishes the results, recipients of the results, and acceptable costs of those results for the entire college endeavor.

The only reason this policy can exist is that the board felt that the broader policy illustrated first left too wide a range of interpretation to the president. Consequently, this policy further defines what the board expects with respect to a subpart of the previous policy example. Of course, the board could have chosen to let "ability and prerequisite academic experience sufficient for entry into a four-year college or university program" be defined by the president. There would be a wide range of possible interpretations that would pass the "reasonable interpretation" test, so the president might well not have chosen the values that show up in the numbered sections of this policy.

Put another way, *someone* must further define the original words. If the board does not, the president has no choice; he or she *must*, for otherwise the college would grind to a halt. By developing this policy, then, the board has decided that it wants to shape the interpretation a bit more itself.

This further policy enunciation by the board still, of course, leaves a range of interpretation to the president and his or her staff. Just what is a "broad liberal arts understanding"? And how much focus does it take for it to be said that this understanding is emphasized? In other words, there are still ends definitions to be worked out before anyone can design curriculum or student performance criteria.

And it is the further definition that would concern a president first, not the development of means to those outcomes. Then after working out the next level of rather broad brush decisions, a president would delegate the fine tuning to staff. If the president chooses to use the same delegation philosophy as the board, the staff would be allowed to choose any reasonable interpretations of the president's words. This book is not about management, so we will not pursue this line of thought. Suffice it to say that the president can use a myriad of techniques to carry the work further, including liberal use of staff committees, participative processes, student groupings, and so forth.

CHAPTER 6

How the Board Operates: Policies of the GOVERNANCE PROCESS Category

GOVERNANCE PROCESS policies are the policies in which the board of trustees outlines what it expects of itself. This category will begin with a very general overview statement of the board's commitment to govern through policy rather than through event-by-event decisions, and the board's recognition that the board "owns" the college on behalf of the community. Thus, the master policy in the GOVERNANCE PROCESS category might read like this:

> *On behalf of the people of Maxwell County, the board will govern Maxwell Community College with a strategic perspective, rigorously attending to its leadership role and the continual improvement of its capability as a body to define values and vision.*

Even though the foregoing statement captures with a broad brush a respectable description of a board's role and commitment, we expect that no community college board of trustees would be willing to leave the description of its own role and process to language as broad as this. Consequently, boards will want to go into further detail about GOVERNANCE PROCESS. While each board can carve out its own particular path in this regard, our experience is that the following topics in this category are usually chosen to be further delineated in additional board policies:

- Board job products ...an outcome or "value added" type of job description, one which details the "products" of the board itself;
- Governing style ...a description of the kind of process or manner in which the board will conduct its business;
- Ownership linkage ...the way in which the board will exer-

	cise its civic trusteeship in connecting with the community;
• Planning cycle	...a plan by which the board will get its job accomplished over a period of time, say, one year; this policy establishes the link between board job description and meeting agendas;
• Agenda control	...the manner in which specific agendas come together, as well as the method by which individual trustees can impact the agenda;
• Officer roles	...the authority and responsibility given to board officers, further specifying the skeletal description likely found in bylaws;
• Code of conduct	...what is expected of individual trustees in terms of conflict, participation, preparation, and general conduct;
• Committee principles	...the principles to be observed to avoid fragmentation of the board and confusion of the board's one-voice delegation to the president;
• Committee structure	...a listing of each committee of the board along with the job product expected of each and the authority granted to each, such as authorization to use a specified amount of staff time or funds.

Policies in this list are, as has been explained, further definitions of the "mega-policy" shown immediately before. *Within* each of these policies, the same level-by-level integrity is observed. For example, in each policy cited, a preamble would address the broadest matter. The board would choose to go into more detail about that preamble only if it is unwilling to allow the board chair to make the further interpretation. (Remember, the chair is delegated the right to interpret board policies which appear in the GOVERNANCE PROCESS and BOARD-STAFF LINKAGE categories.)

Thus, the policy architecture—as with ENDS—assumes an outline form: a preamble followed, if at all, by several numbered points which may themselves (if even more detail is desired by the board) have sub-points. Let us examine two such policies from the list.

POLICY OF THE BOARD OF TRUSTEES

TITLE: Governing Style	**TYPE:** Governance Process
POLICY NO: 2.1	This policy adopted on
	_____ March 1 _____ , 1995.
EFFECTIVE DATE: April 17, 1995	_____
	Secretary

The board process will emphasize outward vision rather than an internal pre-occupation, encouragement of diversity in viewpoints, strategic leadership more than administrative detail, clear distinction of board and staff roles, collective rather than individual decisions, future rather than past or present, and proactivity rather than reactivity. The board will:

1. Enforce upon itself whatever discipline is needed to govern with excellence, allowing no officer, committee, or individual to impede fulfillment of this responsibility. Discipline will apply to matters such as attendance, policy-making principles, respect of roles, and speaking officially with one voice following majority vote.

2. Direct, control, and inspire the college through careful establishment of the broadest values and perspectives in the form of written policies.

3. Focus chiefly on intended long-term impacts on students and community (*ends*), not on the administrative or programmatic means of attaining those effects.

4. Be an initiator of policy, not merely a reactor to staff initiatives. The board, not the staff, will be responsible for board performance.

5. Use the expertise of individual members to enhance the ability of the board as a body, rather than to substitute their individual values for the group's values.

6. Monitor and regularly discuss the board's own process and performance. Ensure the continuity of its governance capability by continual training and development.

Commentary on Board Policy *Governing Style*

The facing page shows a policy in the GOVERNANCE PROCESS category titled *Governing Style*. This category is where the board addresses the why, how, and what of the board's own job. These policies tell how the board will function, how it will connect to the public, what its job output will be, what philosophies it holds, and how it will keep its own discipline.

Remember that in each category of policies, the board creates the very broadest policy first, then augments it with more detailed policies. Moving in this sequence has the effect of giving increasing definition—that is, more detail—to what the board values and how it looks at things. We must assume, then, that before this policy was created, an even broader statement like that shown at the beginning of this chapter had been adopted.

The policy entitled *Governing Style*, starting with where the broader policy leaves off, moves from the general toward the more specific by defining in greater detail the way in which the board will conduct itself. Note that the board created a relatively lengthy preamble due to the "this rather than that" format. Some boards dislike saying what they will not be in this way. Others feel the need to be absolutely clear with themselves that previously common styles are no longer acceptable.

Language in this policy may seem like "motherhood and apple pie" until you notice that boards do not ordinarily act according to this description. When the board engages in self-evaluation, these statements are among the criteria against which it measures itself.

In constructing a similar policy, a given board's values may lead it to different content or to a different depth than in the sample shown. But the policy architecture should follow the sample. That is, a preamble expresses the broadest value on the policy topic. Then—only if needed—smaller more definitive points are added. Even smaller points can be expressed after this by adopting subparts of these smaller sections.

POLICY OF THE BOARD OF TRUSTEES

TITLE: Board Committee Principles	**TYPE:** Governance Process
POLICY NO: 2.6	This policy adopted on
	_____ March 1 _____ , 1995.
EFFECTIVE DATE: April 17, 1995	_____
	Secretary

Board committees, when used, will be assigned so as to minimally interfere with the wholeness of the board's job and so as to never interfere with delegation from board to president. Committees will be used sparingly, only when other methods have been deemed inadequate.

1. Board committees are to help the board do its job, not to help the staff do its jobs. Board committees are not to be created by the board to advise staff. Committees ordinarily will assist the board by preparing policy alternatives and implications for board deliberation.

2. Board committees may not speak or act for the board except when formally given such authority for specific and time-limited purposes. Expectations and authority will be carefully stated in order not to conflict with authority delegated to the president.

3. Board committees cannot exercise authority over staff. Because the president works for the full board, he or she will not be required to obtain approval of a board committee before an executive action. In keeping with the board's broader focus, board committees will normally not have direct dealings with current staff operations.

4. Board committees are to avoid over-identification with organizational parts rather than the whole. Therefore, a board committee which has helped the board create policy on some topic will not be used to monitor organizational performance on that same subject.

5. This policy applies only to committees which are formed by board action, whether or not the committees include non-board members. It does not apply to committees formed under the authority of the president.

Commentary on the Board Policy *Board Committee Principles*

The facing page shows a policy in the GOVERNANCE PROCESS category titled *Committee Principles*. This category is where the board addresses issues of the why, how, and what of the board's own job. Again, we must assume that before this policy was created, an even broader statement like that shown at the beginning of this chapter had been adopted.

The policy entitled *Board Committee Principles*, starting like *Governing Style* where the broader policy leaves off, moves from the general toward the more specific, defining with respect to the use of committees what it means by a commitment to governing as a body. This policy puts great emphasis on the board's acting as a whole. It prevents the board from avoiding its responsibility as a group by farming out subparts of governance to smaller groups. This policy would likely be followed by another that specifies just what committees the board will have, what their expected outputs are, and what each is allowed to spend (perhaps in terms of staff time or dollars).

In constructing a similar policy, a given board's values may lead it to different content or to a different depth than in the sample shown.

Delegating Through the President: Policies of the BOARD-STAFF LINKAGE Category

The BOARD-STAFF LINKAGE category of board policies is the collection of policies describing how governance links with management, including how some of the board's authority is delegated to the staff organization. The broadest statement of policy, from which further definition proceeds, might be worded as follows:

> *The president, as chief executive officer, is accountable to the board acting as a body. The board will instruct the president through written policies of ENDS and EXECUTIVE LIMITATIONS, delegating interpretation and implementation to him or her.*

This policy describes the corporate and written nature of the board's delegation to the president. The board that is satisfied with the level of specificity in this statement will say nothing further. We assume that community college boards will want to be more specific, however. In going into more detail, it is common to create further policies addressing the following issues:

- Delegation to the President ...the manner in which delegation is to occur. This policy establishes the president as the single official link between board and staff;

- President's Job Products ...a description of the president's job written not in terms of the activities of the president, but rather in terms of the unique outputs and responsibilities of the position;

- Monitoring performance ...a commitment to monitor organizational performance by monitoring the explicit policies through which the board instructs the president; specific frequency and method of monitoring each policy is usually covered.

Let us examine two examples of BOARD-STAFF LINKAGE policies, together with some annotations.

POLICY OF THE BOARD OF TRUSTEES

TITLE: Delegation to the President	**TYPE:** Board-Staff Linkage
POLICY NO: 3.1	This policy adopted on
	<u> March 1 </u>, **1995**.
EFFECTIVE DATE: April 17, 1995	<u> </u>
	Secretary

All board authority delegated to staff is delegated through the president, so that all authority and accountability of staff—as far as the board is concerned—is considered to be the authority and accountability of the president.

1. The board will direct the president to achieve certain results, for certain recipients, at a certain cost through the establishment of ENDS policies. The board will limit the latitude the president may exercise in practices, methods, conduct, and other "means" to the ends through establishment of EXECUTIVE LIMITATIONS policies.

2. As long as the president uses any *reasonable interpretation* of the board's ENDS and EXECUTIVE LIMITATIONS policies, the president is authorized to establish all further policies, make all decisions, take all actions, establish all practices, and develop all activities.

3. The board may change its ENDS and EXECUTIVE LIMITATIONS policies, thereby shifting the boundary between board and president domains. By so doing, the board changes the latitude of choice given to the president. But so long as any particular delegation is in place, the board and its members will respect and support the president's choices. This does not prevent the board from obtaining information in the delegated areas.

4. Only decisions of the board acting as a body are binding upon the president.

   a. Decisions or instructions of individual board members, officers, or committees are not binding on the president except in rare instances when the board has specifically authorized such exercise of authority.

   b. In the case of board members or committees requesting information or assistance without board authorization, the president can refuse such requests that require—in the president's judgment—a material amount of staff time or funds or is disruptive.

Commentary on the Board Policy *Delegation to the President*

The previous page shows a policy in the BOARD-STAFF LINKAGE category titled *Delegation to the President*. This category is where the board addresses how it will connect with its executive arm, specifically, how it will delegate, to whom, and how it will assess performance. We must assume that before this policy was created, an even broader statement like that shown at the beginning of this chapter had been adopted.

The policy entitled *Delegation to the President*, starting where the broader policy leaves off, moves from the general toward the more specific by describing in greater detail just what is meant by policy instruction, the delegation of interpretation, and being accountable to the board only as a body. Notice that the president is given a lot of room, but is clearly bounded by "reasonable interpretation" of board policies. It is important that the board be honest about this term; it does not mean the interpretation the board wishes it had stated, nor does it mean what the board's own interpretation might be. The reasonable interpretation rule is critical to enabling the policy delegation to work.

Section 4, particularly in its subparts, makes it very clear that this board is really serious about its obligation to speak with one voice. While the board expects the president to follow board rules to the letter, it frees him or her from having to comply with any board member's or committee's instructions.

In constructing a similar policy, a given board's values may lead it to different content or to a different depth than in the sample shown.

POLICY OF THE BOARD OF TRUSTEES

TITLE: Monitoring Executive Performance	**TYPE:** Board-Staff Linkage
POLICY NO: 3.3 **EFFECTIVE DATE:** April 17, 1995	This policy adopted on _____ March 1 _____ , 1995. _____ Secretary

Monitoring executive performance is synonymous with monitoring organizational performance against board policies on *ENDS* and on *EXECUTIVE LIMITATIONS*. Any evaluation of performance, formal or informal, may be derived only from these monitoring data.

1. The purpose of monitoring is to determine the degree to which board policies are being fulfilled. Monitoring will be as automatic as possible, using a minimum of board time so that meetings can be used to create the future rather than to review the past.

2. A policy may be monitored in one or more of three ways:
   a. Internal report: Disclosure of compliance information to the board from the president.
   b. External report: Discovery of compliance information by a disinterested, external auditor, inspector, or judge who is selected by and reports directly to the board. Such reports must assess executive performance only against policies of the board, not those of the external party, unless the board has previously indicated that party's opinion to be the standard.
   c. Direct board inspection: Discovery of compliance information by a board member, a committee, or the board as a whole. This is a board inspection of documents, activities, or circumstances directed by the board which allows a "prudent person" test of policy compliance.

3. Any policy can be monitored by any method at any time, as the board chooses. For regular monitoring, however, data on each *ENDS* and *EXECUTIVE LIMITATIONS* policy will be gathered as follows:
   a. Quarterly Internal Report for policies 2.1, 2.4, 2.5, and 2.6.
   b. Biannual External Reports for policies 2.3, 2.7, and 2.8. The audit committee of the board will engage the external monitor.
   c. Annual External Reports for policies 2.2 and 2.9. The audit committee of the board will engage the external monitor.
   d. Annual Internal Reports for policies 1.1, 1.2, and 1.3.

Commentary on the Board Policy *Monitoring Executive Performance*

The previous page shows a policy in the BOARD-STAFF LINKAGE category titled *Monitoring Executive Performance*. This category is where the board addresses how it will connect with its executive arm, specifically, how it will delegate, to whom, and how it will assess performance. We must assume that before this policy was created, an even broader statement like that shown at the beginning of this chapter had been adopted.

The policy entitled *Monitoring Executive Performance*, starting as does *Delegation to the President* where the broader policy leaves off, moves from the general toward the more specific by describing in greater detail a very important aspect of what is meant by the president's being accountable. Notice that the board commits itself to assessing the president only against what the president has been told in written board policies. By doing so, the board prevents its monitoring from becoming merely foraging about in administrative material. The board has committed itself to rigor in evaluation of the president. It is saying that whether or not it likes the president, whether or not there are methods or practices used which trustees may not themselves have chosen, evaluation of the president will be conducted only against stated criteria.

Note that the board expects to use little or no board meeting time to conduct its monitoring. The numbers for policies illustrated in section 3 assume the board is using a serial number designation for its policies (for example, the 1.0 series covers ENDS, the 2.0 series refers to GOVERNANCE PROCESS.)

In constructing a similar policy, a given board's values may lead it to different content or to a different depth than in the sample shown. Some boards, for example, add a fourth section explaining how the ongoing monitoring relates to an annual formal evaluation of the president.

CHAPTER 8

Standards of Ethics and Prudence: Policies of the EXECUTIVE LIMITATIONS Category

The EXECUTIVE LIMITATIONS category of board policy limits or constrains the president's choice of the means used to achieve the organizational ENDS. The board has delegated to the president the obligation to achieve (and further define) the ends of the college, and has stated that the president may use any means available to him or her unless they are prohibited by the board. The board may be as specific as it wishes in defining the limitations—remembering to go into detail one level of specificity at a time. As soon as it has finished defining, however, it must be prepared to accept any reasonable interpretation of its words in how the president operates the college.

The EXECUTIVE LIMITATIONS policies are often referred to as the "don't do it list," the practices and conditions which the board would find unacceptable or reprehensible. Because the board starts by stating the policies at the broadest level, it can limit in a general way any means choices which contravene generally accepted standards. The "mega-policy" in this category is often worded similarly to the following;

> *The president shall not cause or allow any practice,*
> *activity, decision, or organizational circumstance which*
> *is either imprudent or in violation of commonly accept-*
> *ed business and professional ethics.*

Note that the wording "unlawful" is not included in this example. Some boards decide that proscribing imprudent and unethical behavior necessarily includes a proscription of illegal behavior. Other boards choose to include the word "unlawful" in their version of this policy. Note also that the policy prohibits the president from causing *or allowing* such behavior. Such wording recognizes that the president is accountable for all organizational performance. Whether or not aware of every staff action, the president must be accountable for all actions of his of her subordinates.

Boards invariably elect to go into greater detail in outlining limitations on staff means before leaving further interpretation to the president. Policies in this category often include the following;

• Planning	...the characteristics of a budget which would cause it to be unapprovable;
• Financial Condition	...the board's list of actual fiscal actions or situations that it would find unacceptable;
• Treatment of Staff	...those circumstances or behaviors in staff treatment that are unallowable;
• Asset Protection	...those conditions, circumstances, and activities the board prohibits in the care and protection of assets;
• Counsel to the Board	...information and assistance from the president and his or her staff that the board is unwilling to be without;
• Compensation	...the limits within which the president will decide the salary and benefits of employees;
• Emergency Succession	...a policy making it unacceptable for the president to neglect to plan for his or her temporary replacement in the event of an emergency.

Boards will develop policies similar to those listed above, and will do so in as much detail as they wish. Since the right to make further definitions is given to the president, the board must be careful in crafting the policies, though it can revise them at any time that the whole board decides that this is desirable. Let us examine two examples of EXECUTIVE LIMITATIONS policies.

POLICY OF THE BOARD OF TRUSTEES

TITLE: Asset Protection

TYPE: Executive Limitations

POLICY NO: 4.6

EFFECTIVE DATE: April 17, 1995

This policy adopted on
_____ March 1 _____ , 1995.

_____
Secretary

The president shall not allow assets to be unprotected, inadequately maintained nor unnecessarily risked.

Accordingly, he or she shall not:

1. Fail to insure against theft and casualty losses to at least 80 percent replacement value and against liability losses to board members, staff, or the college itself in an amount less than $2,000,000.

2. Allow unbonded personnel access to material amounts of funds.

3. Subject plant and equipment to improper wear and tear or insufficient maintenance.

4. Unnecessarily expose the college, its board, or staff to claims of liability.

5. Make any purchase or commit the college to any expenditure of greater than $40,000.

6. Make any purchase: (a) wherein normally prudent protection has not been given against conflict of interest; (b) of over $1,500 without having obtained comparative prices and quality; (c) of over $10,000 without a stringent method of assuring the balance of long-term cost and quality.

7. Fail to protect intellectual property, information, and files from loss or damage.

8. Receive, process, or disburse funds under controls which are insufficient to meet the board-appointed auditor's standards.

9. Invest or hold operating capital in insecure instruments, including uninsured checking accounts and bonds of less than AA rating, or in non-interest bearing accounts except where necessary to facilitate ease in operational transactions.

10. Acquire, encumber or dispose of real property.

Commentary on the Board Policy *Asset Protection*

The previous page shows a policy in the EXECUTIVE LIMITATIONS category titled *Asset Protection*. This category is where the board establishes the limits of the president's authority. Stated another way, in this category the board states the practices, methods, behaviors, circumstances, and activities that it would find unacceptable. We must assume that before this policy was created, an even broader statement like that shown at the beginning of this chapter had been adopted.

The policy entitled *Asset Protection*, starting where the broader policy leaves off, moves from the general toward the more specific by describing in greater detail just what is meant by imprudent with respect to the care of college assets. The board has legitimate worry about care of assets, conduct of finances, personnel administration, and other important aspects of college management. The EXECUTIVE LIMITATIONS category of policies are created to save board time, to prevent unnecessary "meddling," and, in fact, to inject more rigor into these worries about executive "means."

The negative wording used in the EXECUTIVE LIMITATIONS category prevents the board from slipping back into the conventional practice of telling the CEO how to manage. It takes a little more effort at the front end to tell the CEO what conditions or actions are unacceptable. It may sometimes seem unnecessarily awkward, but doing so frees both board and management from unending trivia and uncertainty. This unfamiliar, but powerful approach produces an atmosphere of "go "til we say stop" rather than "stop 'til we say go."

The wording in section 2 leaves to the president the interpretation of "material." If the board is unwilling to do that, it must expand section 2 to describe in more detail just what material means. In constructing a similar policy, a given board's values may lead it to different content or to a different depth than in the sample shown.

POLICY OF THE BOARD OF TRUSTEES

TITLE: Faculty and Staff Treatment	TYPE: Executive Limitations
POLICY NO: 4.2	This policy adopted on
	_____ March 1 _____ , 1995.
EFFECTIVE DATE: April 17, 1995	_____
	Secretary

With respect to treatment of paid staff and faculty, the president may not cause or allow conditions which are unfair or undignified.

Accordingly, she or he may not:

1. Operate without personnel procedures which clarify personnel rules, provide for effective handling of grievances, and protect against wrongful conditions.
2. Discriminate against any staff member for expressing an ethical dissent.
3. Prevent staff from grieving to the board when (a) internal grievance procedures have been exhausted and (b) the employee alleges either (i) that board policy has been violated to his or her detriment or (ii) that board policy does not adequately protect his or her human rights.
4. Fail to acquaint staff and faculty with their rights under this policy.

Commentary on the Board Policy Faculty and Staff Treatment

The previous page shows a policy in the EXECUTIVE LIMITATIONS category titled *Faculty and Staff Treatment*. This category is where the board establishes the limits of the president's authority. We must assume that before this policy was created, an even broader statement like that shown at the beginning of this chapter had been adopted.

The policy entitled *Faculty and Staff Treatment*, starting just as *Asset Protection* where the broader policy leaves off, moves from the general toward the more specific by describing in greater detail just what is meant by imprudent and unethical with respect to the way staff members and faculty are treated or the circumstances under which they must work. The preamble goes into only slightly more detail, but does establish that the board's specific interest (beyond general ethics and prudence) in dealings with staff is the humaneness and fairness of their working environment. Perhaps the preamble would also add, "or in violation of collective agreement(s)" in a unionized setting.

Note that in Section 1, the board could further define the meaning of the words "effective" and "wrongful" but this board has chosen not to, choosing to accept any reasonable interpretation the president chooses to use. Section 2 prevents the CEO from curtailing the freedom of staff to express "ethical dissent" and, again, leaves to the president the definition of how "ethical dissent" differs from any other and what constitutes "expression."

Section 3 is not intended to set out the board's handling of grievances, for this is an EXECUTIVE LIMITATIONS policy, not one of GOVERNANCE PROCESS. It does imply, however, that the board has decided that it will hear grievances, but only under the conditions cited for certain types of grievances. The matter appears in this policy only because the board wants the president to know that hindering staff access to the board under these circumstances is not acceptable (hindering them under other circumstances is).

In constructing a similar policy, a given board's values may lead it to different content or to a different depth than in the sample shown.

Trustees Ask Questions About Policy Governance

In June 1994, nine experienced community college trustees from around the U.S and Canada were invited to participate in a round of telephone interviews. The purpose was to allow trustees to talk with senior author John Carver about issues of importance to them and their boards, particularly the manner in which the Policy Governance model would address those issues. The participants were:

Casper Alessi, Indiana Vocational Technical College
Lois Carson, San Bernardino Community College District, California
Mack Ray Hernandez, Austin Community College, Texas
Ed Hill, Colorado Mountain College
Kirby Kleffmann, Eastern Iowa Community College District
Joseph Lang, St. Petersburg Junior College, Florida
Myrna Popove, Douglas College, British Columbia
Alice Young, Monroe Community College, New York
Allen Schurr, Midlands Technical College, South Carolina

All of the participating trustees were generous with their time and enthusiasm. Each was also kind enough to understand that the interview transcripts would be edited to meet space requirements and to facilitate easier reading. We are very appreciative of the contributions made by these trustees.

The trustees asked a variety of questions about their boards and their roles. They voiced frustrations familiar to all governors about the complexity of the task and the many pressing concerns with which boards grapple. They were both eager to apply the concepts of the Policy Governance model and wary of it as well. Wisely, they demanded information which would convince them that a radically new manner of structuring the board job would help them successfully resolve their very real challenges.

This section of the book consists of edited extracts from these trustee interviews, classified into the four policy areas and the implementational "general" area. In order to make the discussion easier for the reader to follow, we have grouped together parts of the separate dialogues that pertain to each area. Analysis of the interview transcripts showed that the trustees had asked questions relevant to the four categories of board policy making (ENDS, EXECUTIVE LIMITATIONS, GOVERNANCE PROCESS, BOARD-STAFF LINKAGE) already outlined. This is hardly surprising, since the categories were developed to be inclusive.

As in the previous parts of this book, we will use upper case letters when a speaker refers to one of the four policy categories. For example, we will use regular type for ends as a concept, but ENDS for the policy category.

Trustees Ask Questions About *BOARD-STAFF LINKAGE*

Trustee questions in this category related to three aspects of executive delegation: delegation to a single person, delegation from a single entity, and feedback to the single entity regarding performance.

First, the matter of delegating authority only to the president was raised. It is not uncommon for the board or even individual trustees to instruct or supervise persons in sub-CEO positions. Policy Governance holds that boards can get greater accountability from staff by delegating powerfully to only one person—the president, fulfilling a function we call chief executive officer or CEO—who, of course, will delegate further.

> **K. Kleffmann:** On occasion we will have the personnel manager give us a report at the board meeting. I guess we think that that's probably the best we can do to keep the heat on the person to make sure that he or she does the best possible job. But I think we have some board members and especially our chancellor who are extremely concerned about that. It is a concern because you could get yourself in a lot of trouble there very quickly.

> **J. Carver:** Absolutely. Let me suggest a tip. Don't put any heat on the personnel manager. The board keeps the heat on the president and nobody else. I mean don't even look as if you're looking unfavorably or even pushing the personnel manager. It's the president's job to make sure that board policy is followed by everyone in the organization. The board checking on other parts of the organization only gets people confused about who reports to whom.

A further issue was raised about the board's *requiring* the CEO to report to the board as a whole, never to individual board members.

> **L. Carson**: I understand that in Policy Governance some ethical issues can be dealt with by the way the board delegates to the president. The board should make sure the president understands that he or she never has to make a board member happy about anything. The president has to make the board happy, but never a board member happy. We should say that in our discussion and out in the open to the CEO: you do not have to respond to anyone of us in our own personal interests. We should say it together to the CEO.

> **J. Carver:** That's the important part. The board as a body is obligated to protect the CEO from the board as individuals. And what happens is that it turns out to be good management in more than one way. Board members individually have this idea or that idea about programs, or about how to handle the finances or the insurance. It's important that the president knows that he or she does not have to pay any attention to that, but only to the rules laid down by the board as a whole. The president can give the individual trustee courtesy but doesn't have to follow his or her wishes.

Also in BOARD-STAFF LINKAGE, there was a question about monitoring, a matter of great importance to every board. Trustees worry that if they are not right in the middle of things, how will they know whether all is going well? Of course, if the board has not described what "going well" means (in Policy Governance, that is done in ENDS and in EXECUTIVE LIMITATIONS policies), then it is drawn into the middle of things to find out. In a sense, boards don't want to meddle. Under traditional governance, they just don't have many alternatives. When there are comprehensively crafted criteria, however, monitoring offers an entirely different scenario.

K. Kleffmann: How does the board assure executive performance? How do we stay on top of that?

J. Carver: There are two major points in assuring executive performance and they have to occur in a certain order to make any sense. The first step in assuring executive performance is to define the performance that you want. That's an important step boards tend to skip lightly over. And then the second step is to check to see if you got what you wanted. But checking to see if you got it involves a monitoring system that can check the actual performance against the expected performance. As simple as that is to say, that's not typically what happens. For example, boards attempt to assure executive performance, let's say, by going over the financial statement at the end of the month or quarter. They're going over financial data but they're not comparing them against criteria. In other words, the board wouldn't be able to tell you what they would disapprove about the financial statement. So step one is stating the expectations clearly— not blue sky stuff, but really doable things. Step two is monitoring to see if the board got what it wanted. Those are the two simple steps.

K. Kleffmann: Okay, so we put down the game rules and then we attempt to monitor what the CEO does on that.

J. Carver: It isn't always easy, but it is that straightforward.

K. Kleffmann: Here in Eastern Iowa, we meet primarily once a year to go over the performance of the CEO. But I've always thought that this should be a monthly type of thing. This should be an ongoing process. Am I being too tough on the CEO by having him under the gun virtually every day?

J. Carver: I agree with you that monitoring once a year doesn't seem like enough for most areas of college performance. In Policy Governance, your board would set its expectations and monitor some things on a monthly basis. You might monitor some other things on a quarterly basis. And some other things you'd be more than happy to monitor only annually. It differs based on what you're monitoring. Some things are volatile. They can blow up in your face. If they went wrong, finding out about them a year later is too late. So you monitor those more often. In a sense, it comes out the way you said. The president is under the gun at all times.

The president knows that his or her performance is being judged according to criteria known to all and on a schedule which allows for planning. That's what any CEO is paid for, to keep things in shape and to show the board that its requirements are being met. Boards should be careful not to just ask for a report on something without setting criteria first. Often a board will complain that the president doesn't give it enough information or the right information; in such cases it's not unusual to find that the board has never said what it means by "enough" or the "right" information.

CHAPTER 10

Trustees Ask Questions About *EXECUTIVE LIMITATIONS*

A number of topics were raised by trustees which highlighted their concerns about practices and conduct (means) of the staff. In the Policy Governance model, remember, staff means are controlled by the board through policies which state what is not acceptable. Trustees asked a range of questions which clustered around the general areas of finance and personnel. These are areas of college operation which trustees worry about a good deal, and rightly so. There is a lot that can go wrong. First, though, let us see a trustee question that addresses the need for these policies at all.

K. Kleffmann: According to my board's yardstick, we believe the chancellor (president) does a good job and possesses a tremendous amount of common sense. So is it necessary for us to always set down these EXECUTIVE LIMITATIONS? How far do we go? Some of these things are sort of common sense things. Do they have to be said or repeated? I guess what I'm after is a more detailed explanation of these limitations.

J. Carver: The board sets out limitations with respect to the methods and practices of the organization. We're really dealing with a board putting a fence around the executive's authority, if you will, in terms of determining practices and methods. And it takes a pretty simple form really, usually about six pages of policy. For example, the board says that with regard to fiscal management, the president may not allow the liquidity to drop below a certain point. Or the president may not allow the purchasing of items of over, for example, $20,000 without a written record showing that long-term quality and cost have been considered. That's the kind of limitation I'm talking about.

When a board develops these policies, it starts from the very broad perspective of a general constraint. The general constraint is ordinarily as broad a command as "don't do anything unethical or imprudent". Now should you have to say that to a CEO? Well no, in normal discourse, we shouldn't. Except that this isn't normal discourse, it is a group talking to an individual with every person in the room using the words a slightly different way. Besides, the board isn't going to stop with this broad statement. It's going to build more specificity on it. In other words, while a president knows you don't want anything imprudent, he or she doesn't know that you want the current ratio to stay above 1.3 to 1. So the board by spelling these things out assures that it doesn't forget something. And it's the collection of policies, from general to specific, against which you then monitor the president's performance.

Trustees are concerned about many facets of college operation, but financial ones appear very high on the list of trustee worries.

M. Hernandez: How does the board ensure the financial integrity of the institution?

J. Carver: The first step is to define financial integrity. What is the level of financial integrity we want maintained? The second step is to make it so clear that delegation is to your president, that no one can be mistaken whose responsibility it is for maintaining the defined integrity. Boards sometimes delegate so unclearly that you can't tell if the responsibility attaches to the finance committee, the treasurer, the president, or the chief financial officer. Whose is it exactly—as far as the board is concerned? Under Policy Governance you are absolutely certain. The third step is to have a way of monitoring or checking the data to make sure that what's maintained matches what the board defined.

M. Hernandez: We the board are responsible for the financial well being of the college, at least we're told that time and time again. How does that work in your model?

J. Carver: If you look at fiduciary responsibility for your institution, the biggest single fiduciary responsibility that the board has is ensuring that the college produces something that's worth the dollars it spends. That's the biggest single fiduciary responsibility. Is the college producing what it should for the money and other resources consumed?

There's another, more familiar side of fiduciary responsibility, but—for all the attention it gets—it's less important. We focus on fiduciary questions like whether we are getting enough return on idle funds or whether the purchasing system is as efficient as it ought to be. We look at a lot of these aspects of fiduciary responsibility, and so we should. But we forget the one that's the biggest. So I would start by putting those aspects in perspective. Yes, we're responsible for whether the liquidity is in good shape or not. But even more importantly, we're responsible for making sure that this college produces something worth the money it's spending. So you see that the most momentous aspect of fiduciary responsibility is exactly the same consideration that is involved in the board's completing its ENDS policies.

So defining fiduciary responsibility takes place in ENDS as well as in EXECUTIVE LIMITATIONS. That's the defining part. Then comes the measuring part. The board has got to gather the data or get the data gathered for it which illuminate whether those criteria are met or not. So the board's job is not so much doing anything but defining something. The board's job is not financial management, the board's job is the governing of financial management.

M. Hernandez: That's good.... it's something you need to first define and then delegate. Here we're saying to the president, "We're delegating to you Ms. CEO and here's what we've defined as financial integrity. Here are our values." And then we need to gather enough data to see if the return on the administration's work fits with our definition of value.

J. Carver: Right, exactly. Boards get into trouble when they try to help the administration do the financial management because it takes the administration off the hook for meeting the board's standards. And it gets the board off the hook in setting the standards, for if you go do something yourself, you don't bother to set standards that somebody else can follow. Finance committees often fall into that trap.

M. Hernandez: With regard to just what we've been discussing, shouldn't the board monitor the budget, approve bills, review bids, ensure investments are sound, and that our investments are generating a good return?

J. Carver: Those things are all important. Should the board have some way of making sure they're all being handled well? Absolutely. The board is accountable that they get handled well. The board is not accountable for handling them, but for seeing that they get handled well.

So the board needs to state ahead of time what its standards are. The board says, look, why are we interested in purchases? Why do we even care? Well, we care because it is possible to have purchasing in which there are conflicts of interest in the decision. Let's write that down, we don't want that to happen. We also care about purchasing because people can be sloppy about finding the best deal. So let's write that down. Or another worry we have about purchasing is buying something because it's the cheapest, but it doesn't last. So we'll write that down to be avoided as well. It turns out that there are a few very important things to worry about, but there aren't many of them.

In my model the board says: What are those worries? Let's talk about them. Let's even get expert opinion if we want to. We're not measuring anybody's performance right now. We're just talking about what we want to make sure doesn't happen in purchasing or other phases of fiscal management.

And the board then puts those things down in policy which limits the choices of the president. Limits are placed on the president's choices not just regarding purchasing practices but also budget practices and investing practices. These are "don't do it" policies which tell the president, don't let it happen. Of course the board must then monitor to see if they do happen. But monitoring is not a matter of wandering around in a document and asking about this little line and that little line. Monitoring is checking to see if there has been any violation of the standards set by the board. So monitoring is a much more focused thing than approving is. Approvals are what we traditionally do. If we wander around to see if we like something or not, it's because we haven't set criteria and monitored the criteria. Approval is a very inefficient way for the board to control fiduciary matters, including approval of a budget.

M. Hernandez: What is the board's responsibility for insuring that our college is using a fair amount of minority and women-owned businesses for goods and services? And how is that best carried out?

J. Carver: Means can be very important. To a community college, trading with minority-owned vendors is a means issue, related to purchasing. The board may say that it is not acceptable to purchase from vendors in such a way that discriminates against certain groups. The board could even say you can't do purchasing that isn't at least a certain percentage with minority vendors.

M. Hernandez: One thing that I notice our board sometimes does is to go into individual line items and question their validity. We question the cost ..and we don't comprehend the whole. And so I pick one little thing that I may know something about and question it, even though it may be an inappropriate question for me to be raising. But trying to take part in the budget process, I feel as if I've been pressured not to expose my ignorance so blatantly and to question those little things that maybe I can understand.

J. Carver: And I think your experience is repeated a thousand times over every month. The board members are not running the organization and they don't understand all those parts. In fact, the president doesn't even understand all the parts without getting a little help on it. So board members will zero in on this little piece or that little piece. I used to say that if you want to see a group of people get trivial in a hurry, put a budget in front of them. All their trivialities will come out. Just for the reasons you mentioned.

You know the funny thing is that after a board has put a tremendous amount of conscientious effort into going over budgets, you would probably find that the amount of difference they really made in the budgeting was extremely minimal.

Now there's a flip side to that. Sometimes a board will look at a budget and say, oh no, we don't think we ought to be putting this many resources into this or that. But if this allocation were that important, why didn't the board tell the president to begin with?

By the time it's sitting in front of the board, the budget has cost lots of money. It's an expensive document. A tremendous amount of expensive staff time has been devoted to putting it together and now the board is going to tinker with it. Boards in order to keep from feeling like they're rubber stamps will tinker. So they tinker with the budget and then they rubber stamp it. What the Policy Governance model does is put the board's effort on the front end of the budgeting process rather than at the tail end. Let's admit that the budget is an administrative document. It's not a governance document at all.

M. Hernandez: Is it not the board's responsibility to purchase property, approve plans, build buildings, hire the architects, this sort of thing?

J. Carver: I don't have a sharp answer for you on that because it really depends. If you're in a very small organization, then purchasing property may be something the board holds to itself. In fact, it's very common that in the policies that I help boards develop or that my co-author Miriam Mayhew and some others help boards develop, the board places such matters off-limits to the president. It would say "you don't have any authority to either buy, encumber, or sell real estate."

However, if the organization is very large, the board may delegate to the president the authority to make decisions about buildings and real estate. As in other means areas, the board would delegate in a way that sets boundaries; that is, it would state what would not be acceptable about the president's choices in these matters. You can delegate virtually anything if you have adequate criteria in place and a reliable monitoring system. Remember, there's nothing that makes a board or board members better at purchasing a piece of property or designing a building for education than the administration.

Trustee concerns about personnel matters focussed in two main areas. One was around hiring and remuneration practices, while the other was about collective bargaining and general treatment of staff.

K. Kleffmann: An item that is really getting to be a concern of the boards here in Iowa is equity in hiring. We're expected to have people from all cultures on staff, but many times these people do not apply. We advertise and they don't, as far as we know, show up. From the board's point of view, how are we assured that there is equity in hiring as much as we can expect? How do we know we're doing the best possible job with this? The last thing I want to do is go to the personnel office and look at applications. That I really consider is out of my line. But how do I know that the staff is doing a good job?

J. Carver: The board needs to spend some time talking about what it expects of the staff. Are we expecting a certain racial balance or are we expecting that no stone was left unturned in terms of the attempt to be accepting of all races, etc? In other words, what are we going to hold our president accountable for here? Obviously we have to fulfill the law, so that's one standard. Sometimes the board might even want to be stricter than the law, and if it does, then it writes its policies to do that. At any rate, the board has to talk about it. And it has to talk about it from the standpoint of what will we hold our president accountable for.

I think if I were on the board, I would say all right, here we have our criteria and we've set down what we expect. Now, president, we want you every six months to bring us the data that would convince reasonable people who are not expert in the area, of the degree to which you have complied with what we said.

Now it's up to the president to bring the board what it needs. If the president can convince the board that every effort was made to achieve a racial balance in hiring and yet it is an undoable goal, then the board may have to take the political heat itself.

K. Kleffmann: Just what is the board's role in collective bargaining? Our particular board just simply gives to the chancellor, who in turn passes on to the people doing the negotiation, parameters of how far they can go. And that is our only role. We never sit at the table. But what is the accepted method here on collective bargaining? How much should we be involved?

J. Carver: I think you've got a choice. The arrangement between management and people who work in your organization is a staff means issue. It's not an ends issue. And as a staff means issue, it basically falls to the chief executive officer to work out. But anything that is delegated to the chief executive officer is only given to the chief executive officer with some kind of parameters around it. One of those prudence boundaries may state the features of an agreement that the president is not authorized to commit to.

So the board can treat union bargaining like it treats any other personnel matter, that is, it's the president's job. The other choice is the board can say that it itself is taking on collective bargaining as a board job. And if that's the case, then the board when it reaches its settlement with the bargaining unit must give the president another limitation. He or she is prohibited from violating the agreement. So you have a choice to go either way. My choice ordinarily would be to let it be the president's issue, not the board's.

M. Hernandez: How should a board deal with perceived conflicts of interest such as setting rates of pay for different employee groups when a board member's spouse or house mate is an employee within that employee group?

J. Carver: One of the ways that Policy Governance helps get a board out of that spot is by getting the board out of a lot of topics that it shouldn't be in to start with. For example, if the board had to decide which faculty members got promoted, which person gets moved from clerk to chief clerk and so on, you can see that the fact that they know some of these people and they'd be their neighbors in town could really cause a conflict of interest. But the board does not do this decision making itself in Policy Governance; it's done by somebody else. And the somebody else has to follow the principles the board lays down. So good delegation removes the board from having to make event decisions and so removes it from conflict of interest situations.

How does a board deal with salary and wage issues? Ordinarily a board will ask itself why should it set salaries or even salary ranges? It doesn't know any more about salaries and salary ranges than the president does. But it does know what's important to it about setting salaries. It should talk about those important principles and write them as policy. The policy would be a limiting or constraining policy, and the president can be told to set the salaries as long as adherence to the policy can be demonstrated. For example, it might not be acceptable to deviate materially from the geographic or the professional market for the skills that are being employed. There may be other principles to add to this one. Then the board can delegate wage and salary administration to the president, and demand adherence to the principles. A board member who is related to a staff member can still participate in debating the principles by which salaries are set without it being a conflict.

L. Carson: What about such issues as when you have injured parties and these issues make their way to the board? How can the board be assured that everybody from the lowest level in the hierarchy to the highest level is getting fair and equal treatment?

What kind of mechanisms can the board put in place to insure that this is taking place?

J. Carver: Well, like other things the board wants to control, the first job of the board is always to define. A board wants fair and equitable treatment in the staff? What does it mean by fair and equitable treatment? Is it willing to let the president use any reasonable interpretation of that? Or does it want to define that further? It might want to define that fair and equal treatment means that people have an available grievance process by which they can express themselves; that they'll never be discriminated against because of their gender or color or ethical stands.

Then it would say to the CEO or outside monitoring source that it wants to see monitoring data that would convince a reasonable group of people that these criteria have been met. It would also specify the frequency at which monitoring must occur.

CHAPTER 11

Trustees Ask Questions About *GOVERNANCE PROCESS*

The GOVERNANCE PROCESS category of board policy making, in which the board establishes its rules for its own operation, received a great deal of attention from trustees in the interviews. How the board defines its job, arranges itself, organizes its meetings and agenda, and relates to its public were closely scrutinized.

A. Young: What is the board's job description?

J. Carver: I like to think of job descriptions as lists of "values added." In other words, what is different because the board does its job that wouldn't have been if it hadn't. That's a different kind of job description than one which describes what somebody stays busy doing. Our traditional job descriptions list activities, like supervise this, oversee that, review this, approve that, and so forth.

For any governing board there are a minimum of three values added, or job outputs, or job products. The first value added is the linkage or the connection with the people who morally own the organization. For a community college, that's the general public. The board contributes that connection with the public. The second value added is a carefully crafted set of governing policies, the actual paper policies. And the third value added is the assurance of college performance, a kind of public verification. For delegation purposes, this means the president's performance.

So those three things, linkage with the public (in its owner role, not its customer role), written governing policies and assurance of executive performance are the three essential board contributions to the total community college effort. Some boards would add another one or two items to that list of three. For example, a board in one location may add as a board product the achievement of some defined legislative impact. So it's very important for a board to be clear about what its products are so it separates its' products from the products of the college. The products of the college the president is accountable for. The products of the board itself, the board is accountable for.

A. Young: How is the board organized in the Policy Government model?

J. Carver: It should be organized as simply as possible. That means having the minimum number of officers, the minimum number of committees, and focusing the energy of the board on the board itself rather than on parts of a board. The focus then would be more on the total or the wholeness of the board. This makes for better governance.

A. Young: Would officers of the board really be needed under such an organization?

J. Carver: The officer that's needed is the chair. It's O.K. to have other officers, it's just that there is no absolute need for them. Take for example a vice-chair. There is usually on most boards no real job for the vice chair except to wait for the chair to get sick some night so he or she would have to conduct the meeting. If you had to have that officer, you could design a job for him or her; for example the vice-chair could have the job of making sure some part of the monitoring system continues to be working well. So what I'm saying is, you only need one officer. But, if you have other ones, it doesn't hurt anything as long as they're given jobs that do not interfere with the simplicity of things. The law usually says you have to have a Secretary, and the job of ensuring that paperwork stays legally correct is important, but a staff person can do it—and probably does anyway.

The treasurer, on the other hand, has a job that typically interferes with the simplicity of accountability. Who are we holding accountable for fiscally prudent operation, the treasurer or the president? It's important not to confuse the clarity of board-CEO delegation by inappropriate officer or committee assignments.

A. Young: What about the role of the board chair in Policy Governance?

J. Carver: I saw a greeting card once that said a friend is someone who learns the words of your song and sings them back when you forget. That's the way I see the chair. The chair learns the words of the board's song and sings them back when the board forgets. The board says to itself, "We are a group, and groups always have a hard time with discipline. We know that. So what are our rules for ourselves so we will be a disciplined body in order to govern well?" So the board as a body, not the chair laying it on the board, but the board as a body develops rules of conduct so it can stay disciplined and on track. Then, it turns to its chair and assigns the job of enforcing its own discipline. The chair is to be the point person for the board's own commitment to discipline. A good chair is a perfect example of Robert Greenleaf's beautiful concept of servant-leader.

An interesting thing about the chair role in the model, is that the more the board is really responsible for doing its job as a body with every board member being responsible for keeping the group on track, the less it makes a difference who the chair is. Our common experience is that it makes a lot of difference who the chair is. But the reason it makes so much difference is because boards have not learned to be responsible as groups. And when they do that, their chair will still have an important job, the chair won't make or break the board's effectiveness anymore.

Traditional board operation makes such extensive use of committees, it is not surprising that questions about committees came in a number of forms.

A. Young: Now, earlier you mentioned that there would be very little need, if any, for committees.

J. Carver: Yes. I've said committees are often impediments to good governance. But I've never said there should be no committees.

A. Young: Why aren't committees necessary?

J. Carver: Sometimes they are useful, sometimes they are harmful. When the focus is on the board's doing its job as a body, and when the focus is on the board's being clear with the president what it expects as in performance, then the board finds that it doesn't need committees as much. I'm not saying it doesn't need them at all, I'm saying it doesn't need them as much.

For example, you would never have a personnel committee, because there's no need for one. The board will have given the president the standards to be met with regard to the treatment of staff, salary and wage administration, equity, and so forth. The board will, of course, need to gather monitoring data, but they can be gathered without having a committee. There could be a personnel committee to help out in the personnel arena, except that when board committees try to help, they invariably interfere with the clarity of the CEO role. So for a personnel committee

under Policy Governance the reason for existence just evapo-
rates. There is no legitimate need ever to have one.

The same thing can be true of several other kinds of committees,
curriculum committees or finance committees, for example. On
inspection we find that most common committees are really
doing staff work. And in doing that, they are meddling in administration and in fact, taking administration off the hook. Staff,
can always turn to the board and say "Well, the committee said it
was O.K." How can the board hold its president accountable
under such conditions?

*Committees are O.K. if they exist to help the board do a part of its
job. But there should never be a board committee to help the staff
do any part of the staff job.* When you put that admittedly
absolute rule into effect, a lot of committees just disappear. The
board then is left with committees which only help the board get
its own job done. An example of such a committee might be one
that goes out and meets with community members to bring back
certain points of view or a committee that studies the trend in
employment skills that are needed so trustees can better get a
handle on what sorts of community college outputs they'll have
to choose among.

A. Young: So, the board sometimes needs committees, but ones
that really help the board do its job rather than help the administration.

J. Carver: That's exactly right.

M. Hernandez: I know that you generally don't favor the concept
of board committees, however, what suggestions do you offer to
a board finance committee in order to keep it focused on doing
good governance without crossing over into administration?

J. Carver: Well let me correct an impression. I'm not against board committees. I am against board committees that blur the line between governance jobs and management's jobs. I'm against board committees that take management off the hook for managing. And I'm against board committees that fragment the board into little pieces that know a lot about one thing and little about anything else.

But I'm very much for committees for the board when they can be useful to the board in doing part of its job. And there's the key. Doing part of the board's job. Not part of administration's job. So when the finance committee question comes up, I first have to ask why does it exist? What value added does it have? What's it there for? First of all, people are not used to answering that question. And they will begin to answer the question in terms of what the committee does, what it stays busy at. It reviews this and it goes over that. Well, that's not a satisfactory answer. No job is worthwhile because it stays busy at something wonderful. It's worthwhile because it has a value added that contributes to the total and contributes it at the right organizational point.

So then when I push a little harder, they'll say the finance committee sets the budget or the finance committee reviews or approves the financial statement. The finance committee is never using board stated criteria to do this, of course. Actually, if the board had stated some criteria, then there would be nothing for the committee to do but check those criteria. What I've found almost every time is that if I keep probing, I find at least two-thirds and maybe all of what the finance committee is doing does not need to be done. In other words, we've created something which runs of its own accord. The organization would run quite well without it if the board did its job.

M. Hernandez: So we keep coming back to that central theme that you mentioned when we first started this discussion. Is the board activity a value added or is it simply doing good works?

Trustees were interested also in the effect adopting the Policy Governance model would have on board agendas and the frequency of board meetings.

L. Carson: Traditionally, chairs and the CEO have developed an agenda together. They're pretty full agendas and they do get into a lot of detail. Given your paradigm, would the board agenda be much shorter in your vision? What kinds of things would it cover?

J. Carver: *The main thing about the board agenda is that it really must be the board's agenda, not the staff's agenda for the board.* The board owns it, it's the board's agenda. I think if we were honest about it, we'd have to admit that usually the agenda material comes more from the president than from anybody else. So in fact the agenda is really an executive kind of agenda, but raised to the board level. That doesn't produce a governance agenda.

In the Policy Governance model, the board controls its own agenda. It can't do that one meeting at a time. It will end up with a zigzag course if it does. The board must look to the long term, to what it is to accomplish. That is found in the board job description. So the job description can be seen as the perpetual agenda. In planning an annual agenda, the board will decide how much—within the job description—it will commit itself to accomplishing in the next year and it will carve up this plan into meeting-size pieces. In general terms, then, it will decide its yearly objectives with respect, for example, to linkage with the ownership or its completion of its written policies. The board can go into as much detail in planning as it wishes, knowing that when it stops defining, the chair has the responsibility to make further interpretations. This kind of agenda doesn't need to be steered by the president in order to work well. I'm not suggesting that the president be kept out of the board meeting or out of the agenda, I don't think that's right. The president should be there with the board. But if it is the president's job to orchestrate the board meeting, governance simply isn't working.

L. Carson: So you would remove all of those items for approval?

J. Carver: Oh yes, I'd remove every one of them. Policy Governance boards monitor; they don't approve.

L. Carson: No budget items? No personnel items? No curricula items?

J. Carver: That's right. Those important matters can be covered by board policy in a much more powerful way than by the approval method. The board can be far more proactive instead of reactive. And it changes the nature of board meetings. There are fewer items on the agenda, but they're big items. No more endless lists of little items. There are no things the board does just as a ritual action like, for example, approving the financial statement. When have you seen a board disapprove one? So the rituals go away. The content of board meetings is driven by long-term ends issues. The board does its visioning at every meeting, rather than at a once-yearly planning retreat. I don't think those retreats work well at all. They produce a document. But it is not good governance work.

A. Schurr: How does the board decide when to meet and how often? In our case, the board is mandated to meet once a month by state legislation. So we meet once a month as a minimum.

J. Carver: I think that's as unfortunate as it is common. Legislatures do things like that. They prescribe how the board is going to operate instead of what quality of product it's supposed to come out with. Notice that this is the same flaw that plagues the board-staff relationship. As to your meetings, there's nothing magic about once a month. For some kinds of topics, it's much better for the board to meet less often but have enough time to really go into a topic deeply. Monthly meetings tend to become "cookie cutter" meetings, in and out by rote. There's nothing wrong with monthly if it fits the job to be done. And the board is in the best position to judge that, not the legislature.

A. Schurr: From the practical aspects of getting people together, it's probably a good idea to have an established time for your meeting on a regular basis, just because the people will set the time aside. We have 12 people on our board, and to get them all together, you almost need a prescribed something. The fact that they made it monthly perhaps is maybe a little tighter than it should have been, but it comes out. It's not a bad time.

J. Carver: No, it isn't. But my point is not that monthly is bad. My point is that your board should have the right to decide if that works best for it. Rather than the legislature telling every board what to do. It's the same thing as the board telling the staff how to manage instead of telling them the product of the management.

M. Popove: Government itself is trying to manage, which is causing us more and more problems as institutions. How do we deal with that? Can we through Policy Governance be more effective in dealing with those kinds of issues? And will we find ourself in conflict with government?

J. Carver: You may as a matter of fact find yourself in conflict. Policy Governance won't bail you out of these situations. It doesn't change the government's position. But what it will do is it will allow you to do whatever you are engaged in much more efficiently. If you choose to take a strong stand with respect to governmental methods, it would allow you to have a lot more energy left over for that than most boards have now. In other words, most boards are so soaked up in dealing with all the busy work that they don't have much energy to project themselves into this bigger sphere of problem solving. As a result, they're running themselves ragged or neglecting their at-home governance responsibilities. Of course, if government understood the principles of Policy Governance, you might not have to worry about the government's poor governance. But governments don't understand that and can't be expected to understand it for an uncomfortably long while.

The following question relates to the board's responsibility to share its diversity and to attempt to govern ethically.

L. Carson: I wonder how in reality a board might assure that the policies that it develops are ethical, that it's operating in an ethical manner?

J. Carver: You know, I think a way for the board to be ethical and operate in an ethical manner is to really take seriously the need to be in the open, with nothing hidden. Everything must be on the table. I don't just mean things like conflict of interest. I mean how the board looks at dealing with diversity or what the board feels about ethical treatment of staff. In other words, the board must talk about these issues in the open and actually arrive at some very simple and short but written documents that relate to the board's feeling about such matters. The board has to listen to all points of view and make a decision which decrees the standards of ethical conduct to be maintained on the board and in the organization. A group of reasonable people will do a pretty good job of defining ethical standards if it's all on the table, if they must face the stark, public words.

L. Carson: And we really can make what seems to be so abstract, something that we can practice, something we can write about and pursue?

J. Carver: In fact if we don't, we haven't done much more than have a leisurely debating group instead of a governing board. Actually take the values, including values about ethics and humanity, and come to terms with the fact that board members differ about such things. Come to terms with that and actually write it down. Sometimes we tend to think that everybody understands so we don't need to write it down. The problem is we're not writing it down because we really don't understand.

L. Carson: And in talking it through, you do find that common ground somewhere among all of you.

J. Carver: That's the job.

The principle that a board must share its dissent, decide issues, and govern with one voice gave rise to a number of questions.

A. Young: Now, I've been particularly interested in the principle that the board speaks with one voice, or not at all. Would you comment or talk to that.

J. Carver: Let me tell you what it doesn't mean. It does not mean unanimous votes. It just has to be a vote that carries. But whatever carries, that's what the board said. Now that means that the only thing the president should hear is what the board officially said. The president should absolutely ignore everything else. Now, presidents have learned not to ignore everything else because boards are not very good about speaking with one voice. In other words, they will allow a committee to instruct the staff about something, or at least do something that is like instructing, or they will let the chair instruct about something. And even sometimes the treasurer instructs about something financial. So, the typical board gives instructions into its staff machinery through several channels. The board speaking with one voice is very important because that makes good governance possible.

If the board doesn't speak with one voice, than it hasn't spoken at all. The message should be so clear that the board can say to its president "When we speak as individuals, you can take it or leave it. When we speak as committees, you can take it or leave it. But, when we speak as a body, that's law. You don't mess around with that." And it ought to be that clear. Individual board members all have their own opinions about things, and they should have. Where they should bring those opinions is to the board; that's where the melting pot of those ideas ought to be. But if they are able to express their individual instructions and opinions right into the staff mechanism, then the staff is following the directions of a lot of people. Staff members learn how to play that very politically by the way. They will pretend to follow what somebody says, or even hide behind what a trustee says. It is not good governance, and it's confusing to management and it also lets management off the hook.

A. Young: I can see the staff going in all directions, which means going in no direction which means doing nothing.

J. Carver: Yes. And it's hard for the board then to hold its president accountable for what happened, because the board members themselves caused the problem.

L. Carson: One of the things you talk about is the board's developing and maintaining the discipline to speak with one voice. How does the board do that?

J. Carver: Well, it does take discipline. The board has to honor diversity. The second part is that the board must speak with one voice. Now that's a tough job. You must bring in all the diversity you can. In fact, you must bring in more diversity than is represented in the board members. And make sure the ideas, the points of view, the values get hashed out, listened to, argued, debated, fought over, whatever it takes. And then the board has to come to some kind of conclusion. And, with respect to ENDS and EXECUTIVE LIMITATIONS, the conclusion is an instruction to the president. One voice means that the board's values can never be overruled by individual preferences of individual trustees, but it also means that the board has not officially uttered a word until it produces that one voice.

The board's main job is to bring the diversity of a wide community to one point and hand it to the president, saying, "What we want from you is performance. We'll do the politics, you do the performing."

Of course, there was some interest in what a board should do if a trustee ignores the need to act consistent with the corporate decisions of the board. This kind of trustee might be called a renegade.

L. Carson: You have referred to the renegade trustee, and I wondered how the board would handle this renegade. The renegade tends to be an ongoing problem for a board.

J. Carver: The board itself must demand of itself a certain code of conduct. It must sit down and talk it through and write it out. This code of conduct should cover the usual conflict of interest kinds of things, but also cover the kind of renegadism you mentioned, that single trustees or groups of trustees trying to work their will with the staff. I don't think either one of us is talking about the trustee who pushes the board to think harder and has dissenting ideas. That's not a renegade, that's a good board member.

The way you defuse renegade behavior is by fixing it before it happens. If a board waits to correct that sort of situation after it starts, even well-intended effort will be perceived as a personal attack. Most board members don't want to attack another person, they didn't get on the board in order to have fights with people.

L. Carson: And most boards don't think of the renegade until that person has done something blatant or settles into a kind of a pattern.

J. Carver: You're right, and that's why it's important to prevent the situation before you think there's a renegade in your midst. The way you fix it is by strengthening and clarifying the relationship with the president. For example, a board can say to the president very clearly, "You don't have to pay attention to any one of us." When renegade behavior occurs, the president will know that he or she can ignore it, and doesn't have to get caught in the middle. The major protection the board has against the renegade trustee is its relationship with the president.

Viewing boards as trustee owners on behalf of a larger ownership group is a major distinguishing feature of Policy Governance. The concept highlights a confusion that has long existed between customers and owners. A number of trustees wished to discuss this.

M. Popove: Our college system in British Columbia is directly funded by the provincial government. But I look at your system and understand that the ownership of the institution is the community at large, and yet we have to answer to government on all of our funding for most of our strategic direction. I wonder if there's a conflict there for us?

J. Carver: Well there's certainly going to be a practical conflict. Whether there's a theoretical conflict or not, we can talk about. The situation you're in where the provincial government funds the college, but the college board has an allegiance to the local community, is not uncommon for a whole variety of other sorts of nonprofit and public or quasi-public organizations. It's also extremely common for all or part of a board to be appointed by the provincial or state government. I think the board really needs to come to terms with who it's going to see as its ownership. The board needs to nail it down, because in order to talk about board effectiveness, you've got to talk about effectiveness in whose behalf. Often we shortcut that discussion by saying that it's in the student's behalf. But board decisions have the effect of choosing which student groups you'll serve, so there must be a broader base that the board operates from. The broader base may be the government in power or the local community or the province-wide or state-wide general public. The board really needs to talk about this question of who owns the college—it is more often a moral than legal sense of ownership—and come to grips with it. It is not an open and shut case that because the province funds, therefore the province is in fact the owner. The ownership question is not settled by who funds the college; in fact it might be useful to regard the funder as a sort of bulk purchaser, not an owner.

As one trustee pointed out, there can be a confusion between the community, the board's constituency as a whole, and sub-groups of that constituency.

L. Carson: There are constituents and then there are constituents. Trustees respond to these constituents who are over and above them, and they still have to act as part of the board as a whole. How does a trustee serve his or her constituents when acting as part of the board as a whole?

J. Carver: A board needs to reach an agreement that persons on the board who come from specific constituencies are there not to represent those constituencies but, in fact, simply to come from those constituencies.

Now the difference is this. If you represent them, that means some constituencies have representatives on the board and some don't. Because you can't have enough to represent everybody. And it means that the board members somehow are responsible for carrying the message of that constituency almost as if the person were elected specifically by that constituency. And that is putting a lot on one person's shoulders.

Also, when the board comes together, it contains diversity because people have been drawn from different backgrounds and different areas and different geographies and different demographics. But once they're there, the job is to represent all backgrounds, all geographies, and all demographics, so they can do the job better.

Sometimes, when there is a definite constituency connection issue, we let ourselves off the hook for the diversity that the boards have to listen to. For example, if we had a board made up of a handful of people from a widely diverse community, then each one of the persons on the board comes from a certain neighborhood or certain color or certain gender. Does this mean that the board can relax because it has covered those categories? I would say no, the board has not discharged its responsibility to listen to the community. All it has is a person on the board from a particular constituency. That is not the same as finding out about the wide variety even within that constituency. We've let ourselves off the hook with tokenism. So I would be very careful about the constituency board because, ironically, it probably doesn't honor diversity as much as the board should. My remarks apply to faculty and student trustees as well, by the way. There's no reason why faculty members and students shouldn't be good trustees, but they have to remember that the job is to represent the whole community of owners. A governing board is an organ of the owners, not of customers or of employees.

L. Carson: I quite frankly like the idea that our job ought to be constantly interacting with these owners out there. How does the board respond to the diverse interests, pressure groups if you will, among the owners?

J. Carver: Well that's a tall order, but it is the job. I've said that I think it's important for boards to remember that the board as a body represents all the owners. Now each individual board member of course is a person, just an individual person, and therefore has sympathies with certain parts of the owners. It's important though that each individual board member know that being on the board means having a stewardship for the total. And that means the board itself has to deal with its diversity in a very careful way. When it looks outside of itself to the community as a whole, it should reach out as well as it can to tap into the wide range of diversity in the community. That's easier said than done because boards are busy. So they try to honor diversity by allowing people to come talk with them.

The problem with that is only certain elements of the community will actually come to you. Often it's the more vocal or sometimes the better positioned people. They'll come to the board and have their say. But that doesn't represent the total at all. And so I think boards have to have an affirmative action sort of approach to hearing from all the owners. They have to go out to them. They can't wait for them to come in.

L. Carson: So we have to go out and sell this idea of vision and values and ethics and build up this trust of the total community and all of its diverse parts.

J. Carver: I think you have to do that. Now we know that's a big order and you won't be able to get it done perfectly. But the idea would be for the board to work efficiently enough that it has some time and energy to do this other important part of governance. Otherwise the board spends all of its time around the board table trying to look like a board. Going out to the community requires strategy and planning. And it may be best to go out to listen more than go out to talk.

L. Carson: Community forums, if you will.

J. Carver: Yes, community forums or focus groups or meeting with natural groupings, whether they're church groups or school groups or neighborhood groups or civic clubs or whatever else. But meeting with natural groupings of people sometimes is a good way to tap in. Or another way is meeting with other organs that represent the same people, like other boards.

In connection with the board's need to connect with its owners, the community, some questions were asked about the role of the board in advocacy.

C. Alessi: What is the board's advocacy role with the local community, with the state or provincial legislature, and with business and industry?

J. Carver: Let's take those one at a time. What's first?

C. Alessi: The local community.

J. Carver: Advocacy means the actions you engage in to change somebody's mind or to get something accepted or to have something seen in a way you'd like it seen. I think that the relationship the board has with the local community is a different kind of relationship than these other groups that you're going to list in a minute. *For example, the board works for the people who own the community college, the community as a whole. The board needs to speak on their behalf.* So in order to do that, it has to have an interaction with the community and that's not easy to do.

M. Popove: That to me is all encompassing in advocacy. It's a part of listening to the community and taking back their needs and translating the needs and aspirations of the college to the community as well.

J. Carver: In representing the ownership, your job is not primarily a PR job to sell the college and its ideas to the community, but to listen to the community. On the other hand, you have a challenge to help the community develop more advanced ideas about what it does need. So there is a leadership role as well as a listening role. The board that would be successful at both must put a lot of thought into communicating these different roles and into carrying them out. I think the role of the board with the community is just as much one of being convinced (by community input) as convincing, though both are important.

C. Alessi: Now the part about the state legislatures. Colleges and boards are the creatures of the state legislature, so when the board talks with legislators, how much can it advocate, especially when they control the purse?

J. Carver: If a board thinks that something would be better for its community, then it would be obligated to say that, say it to whomever it needs to say it. But it is ticklish. It's important for the board to have its act together to do this very well, so it does-n't look like just one more funded group looking for more funding. It has to show that it is a group which is clearly communicating what a community wants.

C. Alessi: Sometimes the trustees have been appointed by the governor, and the governor doesn't support a position taken by the board. It's sensitive.

J. Carver: I guess you have to worry about biting the hand that feeds you. But it would be good up front if a board asked itself, "Now that we've been appointed by a political authority, are we here to do our best for that political authority or are we here to do our best for the community?"

A board should really talk about that because if it exists to do its best for the community, then it's going to have to say whatever it needs to say. It's not an attempt to embarrass the appointing authority. And if the appointing authority wishes to refuse the board's requests, then that's what it will have to do. Now that takes a rather statesperson-like stance. And yet I think that's probably the right one.

C. Alessi: Now what about the advocacy role with business and industry?

J. Carver: Is the board talking to business and industry about what will be produced by the college? One of the things a board has to confront is that it must know what skills or what insights or what training will allow people to make a living. Therefore it needs to know the job market; here are the openings that will exist five years from now, and here are the ones that won't exist anymore and so forth. And it seems to me that a partnership with business and industry about trying to figure out those things ahead of time is more a customer relations function than advocacy.

On the other hand, if the board is relating to business and industry in order to drum up public, even political, support for another college aim, then that really is advocacy. The ends issue, by the way, is not the advocacy itself, for advocacy is a means, The ends aspect is, as always, the new or continued benefits you are trying to make possible and for whom you want them.

Here is a question asked by a trustee who was concerned about the board's legal responsibilities.

J. Lang: Sometimes a board is required by legislative mandate to decide a matter which is fairly small or trivial. What would you advise a board to do?

J. Carver: If you're required to do it, then you must do it. However, when lawmakers prescribe poor governance—such as approving actions which the board has already delegated—a board should find a way to obey the law in a way that does not impair the integrity of its governance.

In some jurisdictions, community college boards are required to take action on any faculty hiring. Now we all know it's a ritual that they go through, because they really don't hire the teachers and if they did it would be even worse. But the lawmakers have said that's what has to happen.

What I've recommended to boards is to be very certain that they have a system of delegation and monitoring that assures all executive decisions are within the board's acceptable range. If the board is convinced that its system works, it can put the required, ritualistic board action on the consent agenda and get it over with, but spend no energy fussing with it.

J. Lang: The Administrative Procedures Act requires that boards have sufficient information to make an intelligent decision. How does this fit in the model?

J. Carver: There is a responsibility for due care and that includes, of course, acquiring a prudent level of information for making decisions. First, under Policy Governance the board has momentous decisions to make, but due to better delegation, it doesn't have many of them. So while the number of decisions for which information is needed is fewer, the need for adequate information is by no means less.

The board would give explicit discussion to questions like: What do we need to know to make this decision? Exactly which information that we currently lack is preventing us from acting? Where can it be obtained? From whom do we need to hear? The board would get a lot of its information from the president, who is in an excellent position to have access to many sources, but by no means should the president be the board's only source. Trustees' associations, state or provincial government, local experts, and other sources should be frequently used.

For its monitoring judgments, the information the board needs would be, first, whether there is sufficient policy in place and, second, whether it was followed. The second matter compels the next question: Are the monitoring data purporting to demonstrate performance unbiased and trustworthy?

J. Lang: I take note that you say that somebody has to decide whether or not the action of the staff has been responsible and within their parameters or has not been. Obviously the board has the ultimate responsibility. Do you suggest that a board use any professional assistance in making that determination?

J. Carson: Absolutely. The board needs that assistance in some respects. The most obvious is the audit. The audit is outside professional assistance to assess or judge staff performance on a certain part of operations. But there may be other operational matters on which the board gets an outside judge of some sort to make the assessment on its behalf. On other things the board can simply get information submitted to it from the president. That's quite sufficient if it's convincing and clearly unbiased information.

J. Lang: In keeping with that, how about the role of an attorney at law. I would think certainly your advice with regard to the auditor extends to that.

J. Carver: It does.

J. Lang: Many colleges wrestle with whether that attorney should be a college attorney i.e. in-house paid by salary directly answering to the president. Or a board attorney customarily paid on an hourly rate and answering to the board. Any thoughts on that as a part of the model?

J. Carver: Yes. The model would say about that if there is to be an internal or an in-house attorney (or one on a retainer) that is the decision for the president to make and leave it to the president to make. The board has little or nothing to decide about that. But if the board itself wants counsel, it does have a decision to make. Does it have the president make the in-house or consulting lawyer available to it—in the same manner that the president makes other staff available for other functions—or does it want to retain its own? Either choice is acceptable, but the board's controlling an in-house staff person is not.

CHAPTER 12

Trustees Ask Questions About *ENDS*

Policy Governance defines ENDS policies as policies which directly out-line the benefits, the relative worth of the benefits to be produced by the college, together with the recipients of the benefits. The determination of ends is a neglected aspect of most nonprofit and public enterprise. In Policy Governance, the determination of ends, at the broadest level is one of the board's most time consuming and powerful tasks. Here, trustees ask John Carver about this aspect of the board role.

C. Alessi: Where should the board start to focus on the world outside the college?

J. Carver: I would say that's where the board ought to focus almost all the time. The board should spend most of its time deliberating and deciding about the college's effect on the world outside, particularly its effect on the students lives. I'm considering students, for this purpose, to be customers, outside the operating structure of the college. What changes should be being made in their lives? What effect should the college be having on an employment base? What effect should it have for an educated populous? That should be the main focus from start to finish. What benefits? Which people should be recipients, and by extension which people will not be recipients? And what's it worth? And what are the various parts of that worth? And all of that relates to what's outside.

E. Hill: Is that the proper way to develop a mission or vision?

J. Carver: The word vision of course can be applied to a lot of different kinds of things—a vision of how we treat each other and what kind of place it is to work, or the vision about what effects we have on the community and things like that. So, I will probably avoid the word vision pretty much and speak about ends, because I'm sure what that term denotes. The mega-end statement, the big broad statement, is very much like what one might refer to as a mission.

I rarely call it mission simply because I know the word mission brings up all sorts of biases about what a mission should be. Those biases have grown out of approaches significantly different from this model. So you have to be very careful not to develop a mission that doesn't fit into the model that you are using. ENDS statements are very carefully developed and expanded. They might clearly elucidate how much the college exists to produce job skills vs. preparation for a four-year university and so forth. The broadest statement of ENDS cannot include words about the college's services or its programs or what it is going to do. Ends talk is not about "us" at all. It's about "them". It's about what's going to be different out there in the world beyond the community college organization.

So the community input then needs to be of the form that invites people the contribute their wisdom in terms of what is worth doing. You know, what's worth having, what are the dollars being spent for?

E. Hill: So we have to talk about why this place exists. Why is it important? That would certainly bring up a lot of views like, "Well, it's worth having because of education for community people to get better jobs."

J. Carver: Yes. This starts to get at some pretty important ends issues. The next step after getting a high integrity single statement, is then for the board to look at that statement and say, "Are we willing to let our president use any reasonable interpretation of those words and make it happen?" Usually the answer would be no. The board would therefore narrow it down a little more and express its priorities too. It can express its priorities in terms of money, or it can express them in terms of major effort, or it can express them in other ways, but that's the next task. So, the vision is actually built step by step starting with the big statement and adding finer tuning to it.

A. Young: Talk a little bit about focusing on the ends.

J. Carver: Focusing on the ends is something boards don't do traditionally. Instead of focusing on benefits, recipients, and worth, it's all too common to see boards looking into budgetary details, personnel matters, whether we sod or seed the lawn. These are not the things that make a difference in the lives of people, the reason for having a college in the first place. In order to be obsessive about ends, the board has got to get a lot of clutter that currently consumes its time out of the way.

A. Young: Much more visionary.

J. Carver: Much more visionary and much harder to do. It sounds easy but it's really difficult.

E. Hill: It's such a temptation to slip back into the details which shouldn't be consuming our time.

J. Carver: Yes. I think one of the things that makes it difficult to stick with ends, is that board members do have legitimate worries about how things are being practiced. When that comes up, the thing to do is to go back into those EXECUTIVE LIMITATIONS policies to see if everything has been covered. In other words, the board must ask itself if it is worried about something that has already been covered in its policy. If it is covered, the board must be sure it is getting the monitoring data that keeps its worrying down. If it isn't covered, tightening up one of those EXECUTIVE LIMITATIONS policies will cover it. It's always better to make a policy solution than to muddy delegation by setting up committees, or getting more reports. Those are less efficient than using the policy solution.

E. Hill: Do you have any other tips about how boards can better develop these ENDS?

J. Carver: One of the things trustees have to be very careful with is not to slip back into using the concept of goals. There is nothing wrong with the concept of goals, but the way we use the word, there are goals about ends and means. So it's very important that the board use whatever mechanism it needs to keep the discipline.

As simple as it sounds, that will be one of the first problems. Board members will start talking about means as if they were ends. One end is to have a balanced budget. Nope, that's not an ends issue. Or, our ends have to do with the curriculum. No, curriculum is a means. So the board has to really school itself to stick rigorously to the ends definition. Another trap lies in further defining the more broadly stated ENDS. You must avoid progressing from ends to means as you go into more detail. The proper progression goes from larger to smaller ends and never deteriorates into means.

So the board will ask, "What kind of benefits are we talking about". Some benefits are readiness for four-year college. Some benefits are job skills. Some benefits are the ability to use resources. For whom? Are we aiming this at older students? Younger students? People in a certain geographic area? Persons with this kind of handicap? What's the for whom part of this? Do we need to define that further? Now the cost. At what cost? This can be a money issue, but doesn't have to be. For example, we might go after this particular result even though it will cost us a lot in public relations, or even though it costs us the turmoil of having to turn the ship around in a hurry. So cost is really the worth to get a result. The board can put in a time element as well. Over the next two years we want this kind of result with these groups of citizens.

CHAPTER 13

Overall Questions

Some of the questions posed by trustees dealt with matters spanning the policy categories, and for that reason have been placed in this final section. Here a trustee asks a question about implementation of Policy Governance.

A. Young: Now, how does one go about changing over to using your Policy Governance model if for years the board has been accustomed to operating differently and they think quite effectively? What are some of the beginning steps to begin to change over or implement your model? How does the board begin?

J. Carver: I wouldn't even recommend the board begin until it understands the reason for making the change. In other words, I wouldn't make the change just because a lot of other people are making the change.

I think a board has to discuss very carefully why it needs to govern better than it has. Why does it even need to be on the lookout for better models, better approaches? Unless the board is convinced that there is a need for better governance, any changes are going to be cosmetic.

Tom Peters said, "If it ain't broke, you haven't looked closely enough." One of the problems is that we have been able to camouflage governance ineffectiveness in all types of organizations for years. Boards can be very busy at something that looks important, and therefore they think they are doing something worthwhile. But, being very busy at something important, or even having some effects, is not enough to say we've done this the best way we can do it.

North American industry has gone in the last 10 or 15 years through some real changes about doing things better than they've been done before. And the surprising thing of course, is that doing something better is not just a matter of doing what we did before harder; sometimes it is a matter of making a total change in how we look at a task. You can only fix up an old car so much; you can never make it a new car by fixing it up. And that's the way it is with governance. At some point, you have to redesign the vehicle. And that is what this governance model does. It redesigns the vehicle and when the board decides to do that, I suggest they do it all the way. The board must decide if it is worth changing over. If it's worth changing, the board should really change, not half change. It's like jumping from one trapeze to the other; you don't hold on to the first trapeze carefully while you jump. You jump.

A. Young: Yes.Take the risk. And really focus on the ends all the way.

J. Carver: That's right.

E. Hill: When we were in the initial steps of adopting this, we decided to wait until we got the other policies down before we did our ends work. What would be your comments concerning that?

J. Carver: That's exactly what I would do. I would save the ENDS until last. Do the ENDS last because what happens is the other policies, particularly the EXECUTIVE LIMITATIONS policies, take care of the worries that drag the board away from ENDS to start with. So, get those other three categories of policy in place first. Then the board can safely move on the real work, that of linking with the ownership and developing ENDS policies.

Another trustee was interested in the role of the board in securing funds for the college.

M. Hernandez: What is the board's role in fundraising, securing state or provincial appropriations, and getting local taxpayer support?

J. Carver: The board has a choice. It can choose to play a big role or no role in those things. The board can govern fine by simply doing the setting of the policies, and the connecting to the community so it knows it's setting ENDS that the community wants. You could have a board that governs well and yet is not involved in fundraising or legislative activity, but you may not enable as much achievement under those circumstances.

If, however, the size of the board's dream is bigger than the size of the otherwise available revenues, than the board has a choice to make. It either reduces its dream or it finds the funds through fundraising or through political action. The board's answer may be a little of both.

The board must apply the reality of underfunding to its ENDS development process. The immediate question will be, "What are we going to do about the gap between dream and reality?" If the board decides to raise the needed funds, it must carefully define what that job will entail. It may decide to find $100,000 every year or bring about a change in state legislation or local jurisdiction contributions. The board in so doing increases the list of its job products. The board, not the president, is then responsible for getting the job done.

On the other hand, the board can delegate to the president the job of raising the extra money, but if it does so, the board should allow the president to carry out this responsibility without board intrusion—except, as always with staff means, the board can say what methods or actions would not be acceptable.

If the president is to be accountable, he or she should be able to work without board interference. After all, the matter is a staff means issue after the delegation. Individual trustees, though not the board as a body, can still make themselves available to the president or the president's designate to help in the effort. It would be commendable of them to do so, as long as they know that they are at that point, fundraising volunteers, rather than sitting trustees.

So the board can take the job itself or give it to the president, but it shouldn't try to do both at once. It can't have it both ways simultaneously.

Long-range planning is a responsibility that boards have long been urged to accept. Here a trustee asks about the role of a Policy Governance board in this activity.

E. Hill: Shouldn't the board be involved in long-range planning? We're doing our strategic planning right now. From your other comments, I detect that again, we need to be looking at this as far as the bigger picture is concerned and not getting down into the nitty gritty.

J. Carver: That's right. Tomorrow's trivia is not any more important than today's. The board's getting into long-range planning usually enmeshes them right into management work that seems good because it sounds so strategic. It is, however, still bits and pieces. Long-range planning is largely a means issue. The long-range planning should in fact fit the organization to accomplish what it ought to accomplish. If the board has been really clear about what the college should accomplish, then the management can do the planning for how it should get there. So the board does ENDS work with a long-term perspective. Then, the management puts together strategic planning to fit it.

E. Hill: It's very clear from what you've just said, and from what I've read in the book that in fact long-range planning is a means issue primarily. But there's another issue I want to discuss. Our board wants to share this with other boards. My experience has been while serving on a number of boards in various communities both in my town and statewide, that not enough people, city councilors, county commissioners, know how to do board business rather than micromanaging. I'm wondering if you have any advice about how we can share this knowledge with others so that they can develop a system like this.

J. Carver: There are several ways you can do it. The splashiest, and the one that has the highest quick payoff, is to put on a workshop for the community, inviting other boards and commissions. You might even help share the cost with some other people and make a big event out of it. Several things come out of it. One, these boards don't usually see each other, so it's stimulating just for that alone. The second is, the sponsoring organization gets the PR out of having done it. The real payoff, though, is that a lot of people get the idea and can support each other. For the college, a payoff is that if the board of the college tries to govern this way and nobody else understands it, the college board looks peculiar. If you try to govern this way and everybody else knows about it, but they haven't done it, you look bold. So sharing with others in your community supports your own governing.

Selected Publications by John Carver On His Policy Governance Model

"A Model for Strategic Leadership." *Hospital Trustee*, 1989, 13 (4), 10-12.

Boards That Make a Difference: A New Design for Leadership in Nonprofit and Public Organizations. San Francisco: Jossey-Bass, 1990.

"Economic Development and Inter-Board Leadership." *Economic Development Review*, 1990, 8 (3), 24-28.

"Governing Boards Cost Money Too." *Nonprofit Times*, 1990, 4 (3), 31, 37-38.

"The CEO and the Renegade Board Member." *Nonprofit World*, 1991, 9 (6), 14-17.

"Redefining the Board's Role in Fiscal Planning." *Nonprofit Management and Leadership*, 1991, 2 (2), 177-192.

"Time to Junk the Old Formula for Boards." *The Chronicle of Philanthropy*, 1992, 4 (22), 36-37.

"Empowering Boards for Leadership: Redefining Excellence in Governance." Audio cassette program. San Francisco: Jossey-Bass, Inc. Publishers, 1992.

Board Leadership: A Bimonthly Workshop with John Carver. San Francisco: Jossey-Bass Inc., Publishers, Six issues each year since mid 1992.

"When Owners are Customers: The Confusion of Dual Board Hats." *Nonprofit World*, 1992, 10 (4), 11-15.

"The Founding Parent Syndrome: Governing in the CEO's Shadow." *Nonprofit World*, 1992, 10 (5), 14-16.

John Carver on Board Governance. Videocassette program. San Francisco: Jossey-Bass, 1993.

Reinventing Governance: Enabling a Revolution in Leadership for Community College Boards. Videocassette program. Washington: Association of Community College Trustees, 1993.

"To Focus on Shaping the Future, Many Hospital Boards Might Require a Radical Overhaul." *Health Management Quarterly*, April 1994, 16 (1), pp. 7-10.

"Fast Track to Accountability." *Association*, 1994, 11 (3), pp. 25-26.

Board Excellence through John Carver's Policy Governance Model (pre-publication title). Toronto: KPMG Peat Marwick Thorne, to be published 1994.

"New Means to an End." *Times Educational Supplement* (The [London] Times). July 1, 1994, page 6.